Rites of Passage

Twenty letters sent home from Africa between 1985 and 1987

By

Graham Burgess

Thanks for your kind hospitality.
Graham

For my Parents

First published 1996

ISBN: 13: 978-1544910475
10: 1544910479

All rights reserved.
No part of this publication may be
reproduced, stored in a retrieval system
or transmitted in any form or by any means,
electronic, photocopying, recording or
otherwise without the prior
permission of the author.

Design, typeset and all photographs by Graham Burgess.
Cover design by Lyn Davies Design

The moon looks
On many brooks
The brook can see no moon but this
Moore, Irish Melodies. 'Whilst Gazing on the Moon's Light'.

CONTENTS

Introduction	5
Map 1 : Key to Maps 4 – 8	11
Map 2 : Political Map of Africa.	12
Map 3 : Physical Map of Africa.	13
First Letter–*Hoggar Mountains*.	15
Second Letter-*Bangui, Central African Republic*.	25
Third Letter-*Bukavu, Zaire*.	33
Fourth Letter-*Kenya/Tanzania Border*.	38
Fifth Letter-*Tanga,Tanzania*.	52
Sixth Letter-*Maun, Botswana*.	67
Seventh Letter-*Victoria Falls, Zambia*.	74
Eighth Letter-*Victoria Falls, Zambia*.	85
Ninth Letter-*Maun, Botswana*.	95
Tenth Letter-*Near Kigali, Rwanda*.	110
Eleventh Letter-*Bakavu, Zaire*.	117
Twelfth Letter-*Near Douala, Cameroun*.	138
Thirteenth Letter-*Kano, Nigeria*.	146
Fourteenth Letter-*The northern Sahara Desert*.	159
Fifteenth Letter *Rabat, Morocco*.	179
Sixteenth Letter-*The Southern Sahara Desert*.	194
Seventeenth Letter-*Cotonou, Benin*.	205
Eighteenth Letter-*North-West Cameroun*.	210
Ninteenth Letter-*Near Businga,Zaire*.	224
Twentieth Letter-*Ngorongoro Crater, Tanzania*.	238
Postscript.	260
About the author	263

INTRODUCTION

I was 26 years old at the time I embarked upon the following adventures, bright-eyed and, in hindsight, rather naïve. The subsequent two years brought about a vast widening of perspectives in many fields: cultural, personal, organisational, not to mention geographical. My faculties for making sense of these new vistas were forced into a trot in order to keep up. (The bleached bones of many a sacred cow lie abandoned in the desert!). This process of a changing and maturing outlook is readily apparent through the letters home that follow.

It all began in the summer of 1985, when I met a friend in Bristol I had not seen for several years. I asked him what he he'd been doing and he told me that he'd recently started a job that was to involve driving lorry-loads of tourists to Nepal. Now, I had already considered taking a PSV driving test to try to get a job with 'Magic Bus' or some other such outfit providing budget travel to exotic destinations. The trouble with most of these, however, was that they were straight A to B travel – not so much sightseeing on the way. 'Exodus Expeditions', the company my friend was working for, on the other hand, specialised in 'adventure holidays' (though, as we were often to point out, it never actually said 'holiday' in any part of their literature!). This meant that they would be visiting interesting places on the way and camping each night on trips lasting often several months. Needless to say, I eagerly asked for the address and applied for a job as 'expedition leader'. The process was fairly involved, beginning with an interview at the workshop in Wiltshire, followed by a week-long 'assessment'. This consisted in being given all the most horrible jobs and having to sleep in a damp and greasy bedroom with access to little more than a cold shower (which needed pliers to turn it on!). The purpose of all this was presumably to see whether applicants were suited to 'third world' conditions! This accomplished, I was given a date on which to report back to the same workshop for 'training'. I was lucky, firstly in that I already held an HGV licence – others had to take one as part of their training -; and secondly, in that I already had wide mechanical experience, these being, at this stage, the primary prerequisites for the job.

I returned, then, to the workshop for about six weeks, and was initially given diverse work to do. Alan, the workshop manager, had no idea where I would be sent and suggested that I begin to read up about all the places where I *might* be sent. As this covered Asia as far as Nepal and India, the whole of South America, and at least three possible routes through Africa, I read little. Then one day I was called into the office and told that I was to be sent on a Southbound 'Trans-Africa' trip two weeks hence, and that I had better sort out the relevant vaccinations. From this point onwards, my work was exclusively directed towards building the vehicle which we were to rely on for the next five months or so. "Have you ever assembled a commercial synchromesh gearbox?" I was asked by Alan one day. I told him I hadn't. "Well" he said, "the gears are in this box, the casings are over there on the floor and the instruction manual is in the cupboard. Let me know when you've finished". It took three attempts, but once I'd done it, I knew exactly how it all worked and was confident that it wouldn't let us down. (It didn't.)

The vehicles used for the African expeditions were ex-army four-wheel-drive Bedford MK lorries. These were fitted with lockers and two long bench seats in the back. The sides of the plastic tarpaulin canopy could be rolled up so that the passengers were effectively sitting in the open air. Those wanting even *more* open air would be able to use the 'safari seat' (or 'dog-box'), which was an open, forward-facing seat, the full width of the truck just above and behind the cab. The vehicles were fitted with storage for a good deal of dried food (though this was for emergencies and the desert; expeditions being expected to buy food locally en route). We carried a fairly comprehensive selection of spare-parts and a good tool-kit. Fastened to the outside were spare leaf-spring sets for the suspension and four 'perforated steel planks' for use as sandmats in the desert. Underneath were diesel tanks with a total capacity of two-hundred-and-fifty gallons. On the roof of the cab were stored ten two-man tents and a large awning for use as a 'cook-tent' in bad weather. Two trestle tables slid in above the fuel tanks, and twenty-two folding stools, behind the mudguards. A one-hundred gallon water tank was fastened to the chassis behind the cab, with space above for firewood that might be collected on the way. We even found space for a camp oven and a 'library'!

The first trip that anyone does is as a 'trainee'. This means that, although you do half the driving, the expedition is run by another employee who will have done the route at last once before. The expedition leader on my 'training trip' was Paul Mercer, a 29 year-old Welshman who had done just one trip before – *his* training trip.

On the day we left, we drove to Portsmouth to meet the group who had been brought by coach from London; there was to be a full group of twenty, including some to be picked up in Paris. We bustled about organising luggage and people, and I tried to appear confidently official – whilst feeling distinctly unsure of the procedures. Soon enough we were on our way to the big adventure...

The letters began as simply letters home to my family. But, as any traveller will tell you, it soon becomes a chore to write accounts of the same events separately to several people. I suggested to some people that, if they were interested, they could visit my parents in order to get a fuller account than I could write on a postcard. What I did not know – at least not for the initial few weeks – was that it was not only a few friends and relatives that had taken to reading my letters, but also relatives of friends and friends of relatives! My mother had begun typing-out and photocopying each instalment for circulation. By my third or fourth letter, I had become aware that I was writing to an audience of several dozen people, many of whom I had never met. This presented a new and exciting challenge – how to re-create, in the imagination of my readers, an experience akin to that of being in Africa when I knew that most of the people probably never had, and probably never would, actually go there. I was well aware that I could not *give* people my experiences, but wondered whether I may possibly act as a catalyst for some imaginary experiences of their own.

I am indebted to several of these readers for their encouragement towards my transforming what was a scruffy typescript tied together with string into this book. Thanks especially to my mother for the original typing and distribution, to Viv Versis for subsequently typing it for this edition. Thanks also to all those who wrote replies to me, both in Africa and since, as well as to those others whose encouragement persuaded me to further explore the world of writing. Thanks finally to David Barnett and his wife Paula for their generous and expert advice.

G.P.B April 1996, Cardiff

Graham Burgess in 1986

- RITES OF PASSAGE -

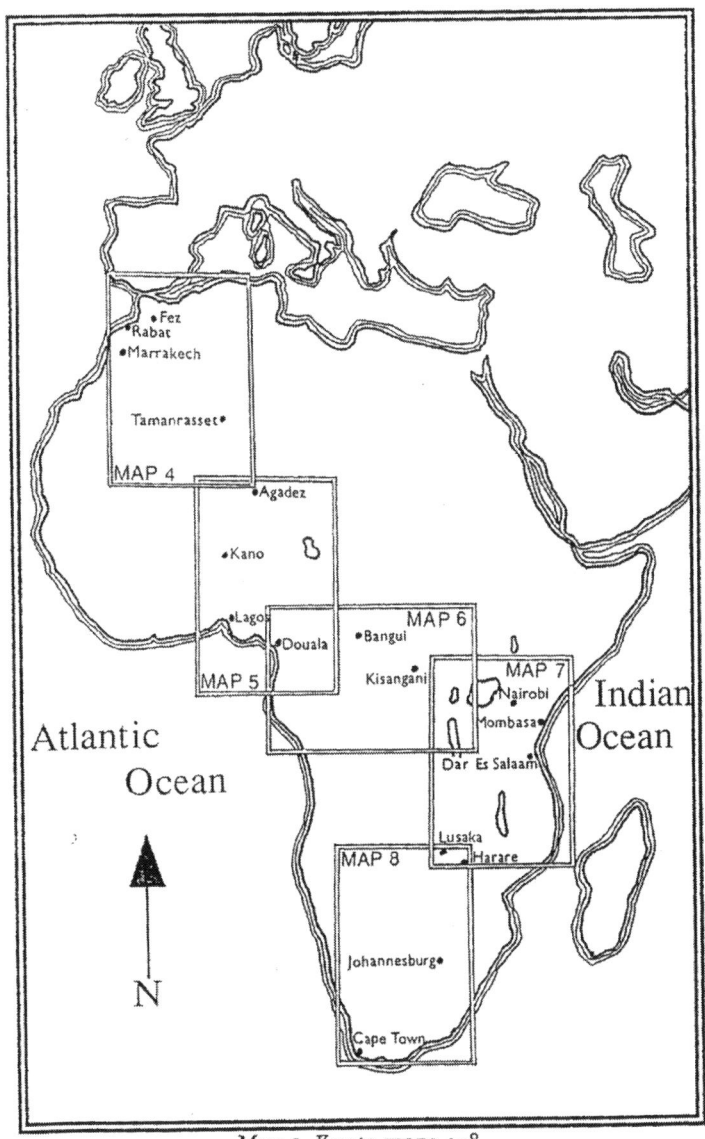

Map 1. Key to maps 4–8.

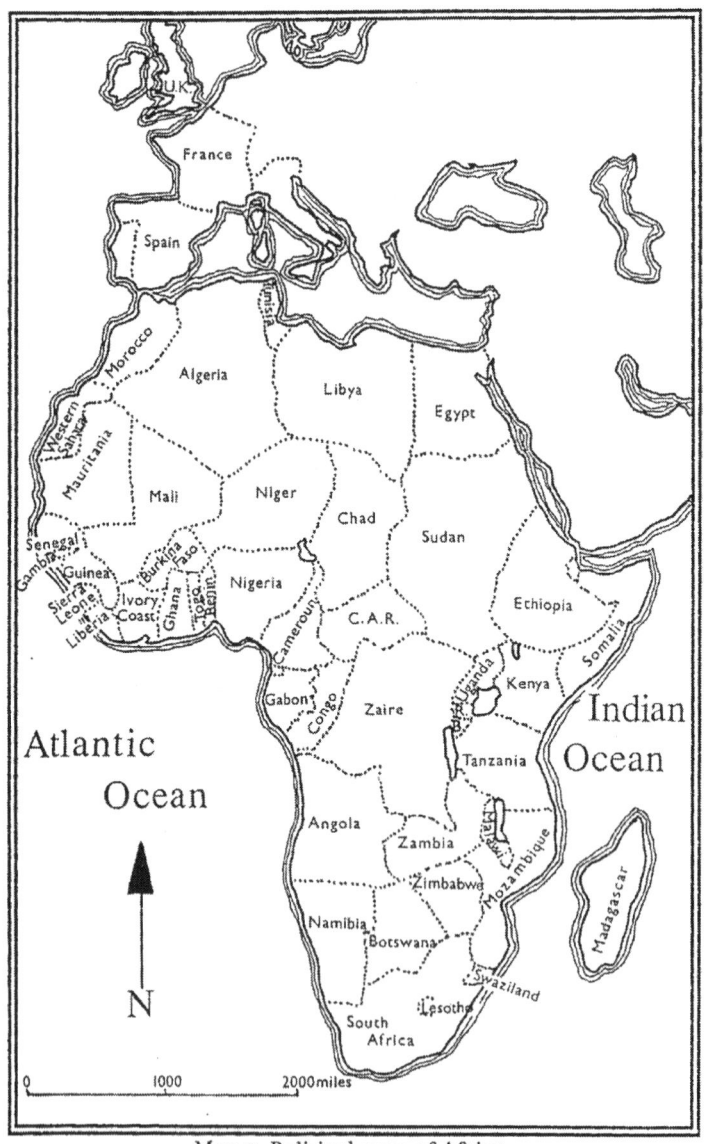

Map 2. Political map of Africa.

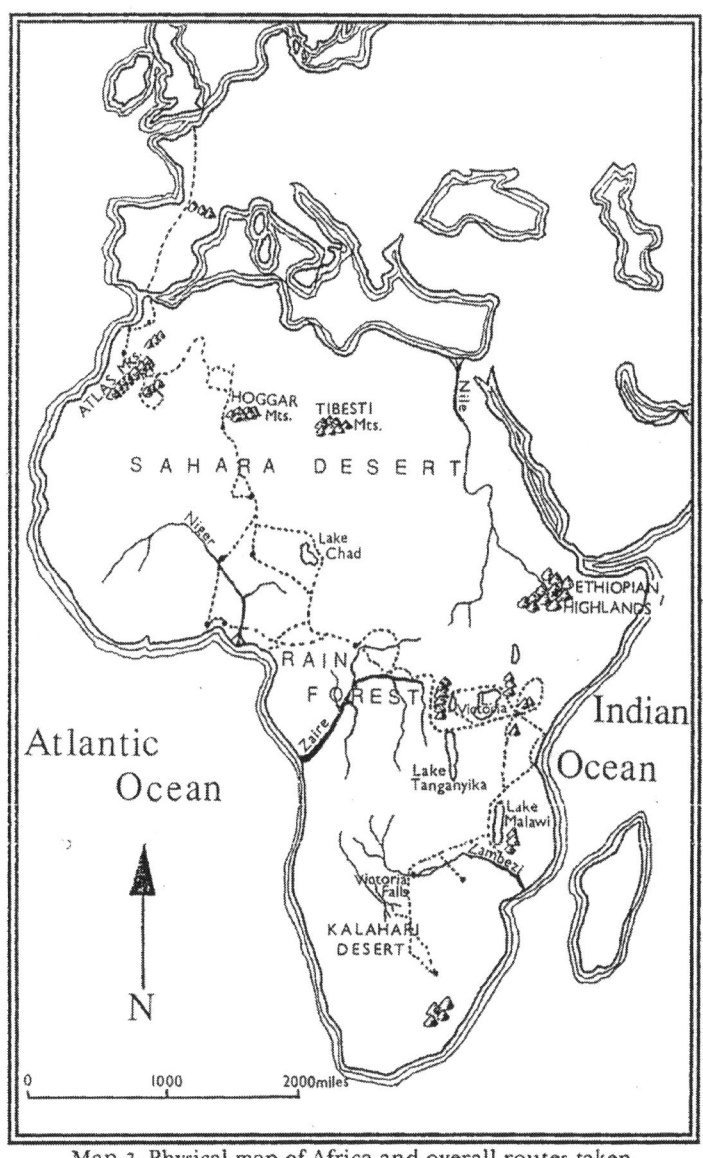

Map 3. Physical map of Africa and overall routes taken.

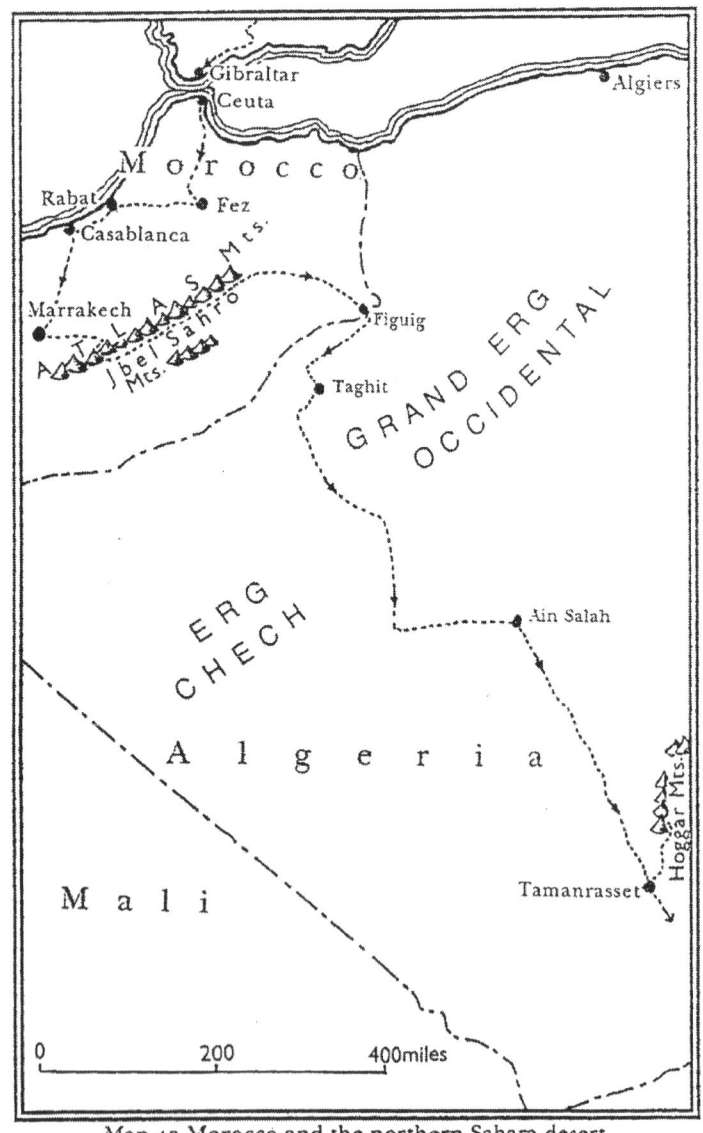

Map 4a. Morocco and the northern Sahara desert.

28th November 1985

Dear All,

Well, here I am at the top of the Hoggar Mountains in the central Sahara. It certainly is magnificent. The sun has just set red and the huge yellow moon arisen.

Where do I start? Morocco I think. We didn't stop for long at the smaller towns of northern Morocco though at the first one I found it friendly and strange to see the men in striped djalabas with pointed hoods, like Hobbits! The women cover their faces but that doesn't stop them from flashing their eyes sometimes!

The border had been chaotic and disorganised. Some say it's designed that way to discourage travel. The roads were fair for the most part, single track asphalt with wide gravel edges which you must drive on to should anyone come the other way or want to overtake.

Driving down towards Meknes we stopped at some extensive Roman ruins called Volubilis. Unfortunately, I knew nothing about it, and even though it was well-preserved, it meant little to me.

That night we arrived at Fez camp site. There were several other overland vehicles, though none from Exodus. Paul said that he knew of a nearby Hammam (Turkish bath) so we set off armed with towels to find it. It was closed but we were told of another, and, after a fairly long walk, found it. They didn't want to let us in as it seemed they were closing but, after a while, they agreed. Women in one side, men in the other, we were shown into a large tiled echoing room and told to undress. Paul had said that at the other baths they didn't allow nudity so we had all taken our trunks. We started undressing while at least an equal number of Moroccan men, employees of the baths, came in and also started to undress.

"We massage très bien" said one: they were all laughing and the echoes boomed around the chamber. We all looked at each other uneasily, slowly pulling off jackets, shirts, trousers. "What are we doing here?" one of our group mouthed at me.

Not wanting to leave valuables with my clothes, I stuffed £30 worth of Moroccan money and my watch down my trunks and followed the others through another large hot chamber into a third. This one had a floor so hot it was hard to stand on it. In one corner was a trough of hot water, in the opposite corner a trough of cold. Buckets were lying around so we all started to wash.

Two members of our group were soon grabbed and made to lie on the floor and be washed and massaged. We were all very dubious. Some declined but most succumbed as it seemed okay. It actually felt great. I was twisted and turned, washed, scrubbed, massaged, and we all felt completely revitalised. After the massage the masseur threw several buckets of cold water over me and all I could think of was all that soggy money and wet watch in my trunks.

Back at the campsite we had three eager guides for the next day's tour of the town. It is better to arrange a guide as otherwise you will inevitably pick up several more unscrupulous guides who will squabble amongst themselves to lead you – and are only usually interested in leading you into shops where they'll get commission on goods you may buy.

The next day 'Abdul' and 'Baba Ahmed' rode in the truck to town and we began one of the most memorable days so far (or even ever). If anyone wants to know what medieval English towns were probably like – come to Fez. Narrow streets, passages, alleys, tunnels, covered markets, donkeys and mules galore. Streets full of tiny rooms, maybe six feet square, fronted with large wooden doors – the shops and workshops. Metalworkers hammer metal, leatherworkers make shoes, knife sharpeners sharpen knives on pedal-powered machines. It is impossible to convey the atmosphere of the place. Haggling for a reasonable price is not only expected but fun. After all, the chances are that every other shop in the street sells the same thing. You supposedly have to walk out three times – they always call you back, sometimes they'll run after you and haggle in the street. I was fascinated and would love to spend more time there.

Two of our passengers, an Australian girl and an American girl, didn't have visas for the Central African Republic so I had to take them to Rabat, the capital, to obtain them. The train was slow, with wooden seats and the journey took five hours but was, nevertheless, enjoyable. Everyone who sat with us, and there were several, was really friendly and even gave us addresses. My French is rapidly improving through necessity!

Rabat is a pleasant town, clean and without the bustle and hard-sell of Fez. We were there for three days, after which we got the necessary visas. We were befriended by a Moroccan guy of about my age. He knew Rabat well and showed us round, haggled for us in Arabic and spoke very good English. We also met an English couple and we all went out for a meal two nights running.

We found out train times to Marrakech and caught the Marrakech Express. It turns out that 1985 is the first year that such a thing has existed so the song was a little before its time. The train was comfortable, fast, but relatively expensive. The one from Fez to Rabat had cost about £1.60; this one was more like £5 each.

The English couple we met also travelled with us and we all booked into a hotel in Marrakech when we arrived at about 10.30pm. The next morning we walked towards the centre and caught a horse-drawn taxi – the very worst way to enter the Square in Marrakech. We alighted and suddenly had three guides and lots of hasslers. We escaped the guides and started walking near some snake-charmers. Next thing I had a snake wound round my neck and a bloke demanding money for the photographs the others were taking of me. Luckily we soon found the truck and the rest of the group who had booked into a hotel in the centre. After having time to recover, I braved the Square again and thoroughly enjoyed it. That night it poured down; Marrakech is as unprepared for rain as Taunton is for sandstorms and soon the narrow streets were ankle deep in water.

The next day we headed off towards the Atlas Mountains through palm trees and sunshine. The mountains soar way above the snowline. The many small earth and rock-built villages seem to grow out of the ground and are almost invisible until you are upon them.

The scenery is spectacular and the air cold. People are selling lumps of amethyst all along the road and even stand in the road holding lumps into the air.

Over the mountains around twisting hairpins; the landscape becomes more arid and deserted. Driving over wide plains, past bare mountains and ever more infrequent habitation, we spent a night at the Gorges du Todra, a remote and impressive canyon with a warm river. In the morning we had plenty of time to look around the nearby town, Tinerhir, a mud built Kasbah town with an interesting market and extremely friendly people.

We eventually made it to the Algerian border at Figuig and predictably it took all day to get through. We had the truck searched three times and it cost us altogether two half bottles of whisky, sixty cigarettes and three cassette tapes distributed between the Moroccan police, customs and border guards, and the Algerian border guards. They must do all right as they routinely ask for bribes and most people have come prepared for this.

At the border we met two Englishmen from Lynton crossing the Sahara in a Peugeot 504. We've seen them several times since.

We headed south from here towards Bechar and then left to Taghit. Taghit is in a fantastic setting; huge sand-dunes rise up behind this mud town which is surrounded by palm trees. 18km further on, the road ends facing a crumbling cliff face on which are many very well-preserved prehistoric rock engravings. Clearly portrayed are gazelle, buffalo, elephants and ostriches. Looking out over today's scene it's hard to believe that this now barren land could have supported such life. It is known, however, that the Sahara had a Mediterranean climate until about 4000 years ago. Though contrary to popular opinion it is not simply the fault of humans that the desert is expanding – as it is also known that in earlier times it has been far larger than it is even now.

The daytime sun gets hotter every day - though to confirm the popular myth, the nights can be very cold especially just before sunrise, when the temperature seems to drop suddenly. We get up at 6 am every day so always see the sunrise.

We continued down past Beni-Abbes to Adrar where the passengers had to change money. The official exchange rate is dreadful as it is a closed economy making everything here very expensive indeed. Also everyone has to change a minimum of 1000 dinar (about £150) and it is illegal to bring any out of the country. And then onwards towards Reggane where we turned left towards Ain Salah along an unknown road. Paul had not been this way before. It started off OK but soon deteriorated into deep corrugations and potholes.

Eventually at the scene of several road-making machines it petered out completely leaving us to follow a few tyre tracks in soft sand. I soon found that in such circumstances you must not drive in someone else's tracks as the sand is softer there, so I had to break new ground all the time. It really felt like the wilderness now, especially after we kept getting bogged down, having to use sand-mats; that is, heavy perforated steel planking, for hours at a time.

Later we found a reasonable track marked by occasional piles of stones but this soon led into sandy troughs. Also we were constantly faced with alternative tracks forking off this way and that. I supposed they'd all end up at the same place. Luckily they did – and after passing two artesian wells and two oases, we arrived in Ain Salah. It was the eve of Mohammed's birthday, the equivalent of Christmas Eve so there was much singing and dancing all night.

The next day we drove south on the three day trek to Tamanrasset. The first 60km is quite a good tar road but after this it breaks up into huge potholes and ruts. There are frequent by-pass tracks in the sand and it is often easier to drive over the corrugated sand than to slowly weave amongst the potholes. That night we stopped at Arak Gorge. From here is a good road that is forbidden as it was constructed by the army for its own use. We had 300km of rocks, boulders, soft sand and corrugations to negotiate – frustratingly crossing and re-crossing the tarmac road occasionally guarded by soldiers. The driving was hard work and the next day we covered little more than 150km. The last 80km to Tamanrasset is on the tarmac so we got there at 5pm on Wednesday 27th November. It was nice to find I had two letters waiting for me at the post-restante.

Another truck was also in town and we later met up at the campsite. Next day I went with a group of fifteen from both trucks up to the Hoggar Mountains.

We travelled in local four-wheel drive vehicles organised through the tourist office. It would be a long hard road for our trucks but fairly easy in these.

The drivers were good and stopped frequently for photos or at interesting places. We got to the top where there is a stone refuge and, after unloading our sleeping gear, the red sun sank behind the silent basalt moonscape and I felt strangely at home here in the world. Back at the refuge our Tuareg hosts were preparing dinner. The food was good and there was plenty – it was even mainly vegetarian.

I arose at 5am and climbed back up the mountain to watch the sunrise. There had been five people sleeping at the top – I would have joined them had I known how stuffy the refuge was going to be. After breakfast of bread, jam and coffee we drove back at a leisurely pace and had a lazy afternoon at the campsite. Tomorrow we must clear customs and head on down to the Niger border.

Our truck is the best organised of any we've met so far (we've met three). Everyone has their jobs (mine, of course, being vehicle maintenance) and the passengers take turns at shopping, cooking and washing-up in pairs. So far we're all getting on fine. We have far more medical advice, expertise and equipment than I hope we could ever need.

Paul and I take turns driving – an afternoon and following morning each. Whilst not driving we each sit in the back and one of the passengers has a choice of a good view, heat when it's cold, dust-free air and music. We've started using the open seat above the cab now it's warmed up so the suntans are doing fine!

The passengers – eleven men, eleven women, including Paul and I – consists of Australians, New Zealanders, Canadians, two Dutchmen (one a customs officer and group joker), an American and various English. Their ages range from nineteen to about forty-five. We have students, nurses, a hotelier, a geologist, and an artist to name a few. It can be difficult sometimes to get some of them to take an interest in where they are but it's getting better now that they sometimes have to run around with steel sandmats and breathe in thick dust or get sand between their teeth! We've all bought the local headgear which is extremely practical, keeping hair dust-free and shaded and having a built-in dust mask.

So far, illnesses amongst the group have been limited to coughs and colds plus an occasional bout of diarrhoea but, for me, so far so good.

By the time you get this I should be in Bangui in Central African Republic; we hope to spend Christmas there. I'll try and phone.

Until then,
Happy Christmas,

Love,
Graham.

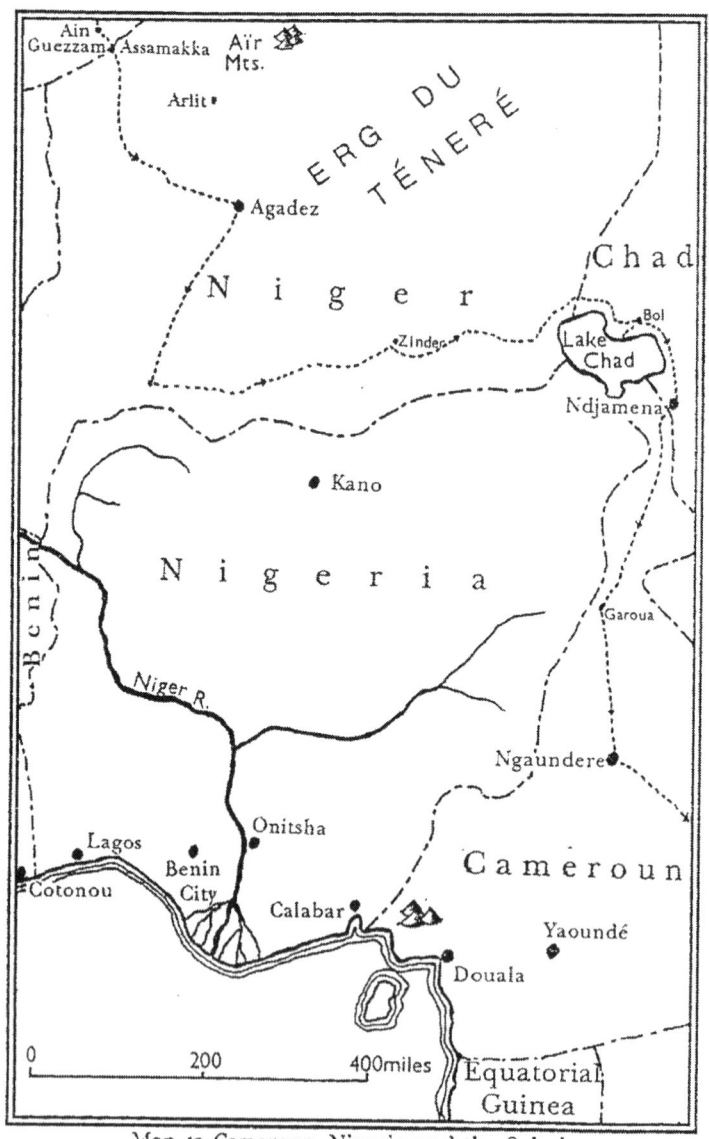

Map 5a. Cameroun, Nigeria and the Sahel.

24 December 1985

Dear Mum, Dad, Mal and Ruz

Thanks for your letters, you're right, it is nice to get letters from home. I got seven yesterday so I've got a lot of writing to do! Well, to commence: we left Tamanrasset and drove south, the road is good for 40 miles but then runs out. From here it is rough piste. At length we reached Ain Guezzam and met two other Exodus trucks waiting to go through the border. We had to camp the night and go through next day.

Assamakka, the gateway to Niger, is a small collection of mud huts and tents in the middle of the desert. There are no roads going to or from it; only tyre tracks in the deep sand and a line of oil drums, 1km apart to mark the route south.

After a further long day's driving the desert gives way to scrub and, rapidly, scrub to greenery. There is a fair amount of agriculture – mainly maize and cassava. The people are beautiful, dressed in vivid colours and always smiling and friendly. Everywhere we go we are continually waving and when we stop, attract crowds of wide-eyed children.

From Assamakka we took the back road (by accident) through Tegguidda-a-Tessoum to Agadez and from here drove southwest to Tahoua, Maradi, Zinder, Goure, Diffa and Nguigi to cross to Chad, back into the desert, Nigeria's land borders being presently closed to foreigners. To cross the border from Nguigi to Daboua involves a five hour drive on compass bearings on very soft sand. We let our tyres down to 45 psi to make it easier but still often get stuck. Our first taste of Chad was to be our impression to the end.

On the border children have automatic rifles, the 'police' and customs are interested only in what you may give them and it cost us half a bottle of whisky, a couple of cassettes and a few packets of cigarettes to get through. Most of Lake Chad has been dry for the last ten years, there are no roads around it so it's a question of using the compass, the sun and a few tyre tracks of previous vehicles. There are also several military checkpoints to be negotiated. At these places there is a lot of gun-waving and bribing – more cigs, cans of diesel, T-shirts etc., etc. At one we were given no choice but to give two armed soldiers (one a 'commandant', the other with his entire head concealed by a 'shesh' and his eyes by mirror shades, looking like a terrorist), a lift to Bol. We ended up taking a wrong turn and found ourselves at Baga Sola near a part of the remaining lake where we were forced to endure yet another full vehicle search.

Our military guests were strangely absent until this was done – but afterwards made it abundantly clear that they wanted to get to Bol that night. The sun soon set as we struggled across deep soft sand, up steep slopes on a compass bearing.

They insisted we drive into the night but we'd all just about had a bellyful by this time. Paul and I decided to pull the engine stop knob at the next good spot to make out we'd broken down. We didn't have to. After getting bogged down on a steep incline there was a loud BANG! Our rear differential broke up. Paul and I spent much of the night under the truck replacing it, keeping a wary eye out for scorpions as the place was alive with them. In the morning our soldier friends recruited the help of a local village who effectively deforested an area to lay a branch and bush 'road' for us. One woman in the group foolishly decided to sneak a photograph but these are strictly forbidden and the soldiers later told the police who confiscated her camera. It took most of the day to get to Bol. We had to sandmat for hours at a time in the blazing heat and also had to have the cab heater on as the engine was overheating. It must have been 120º in there and tempers were getting short.

Next day in Bol, after a few formalities, we had to be searched by 'police'. They rummage through everyone's gear picking out so-called 'military' items which they say are forbidden. They're not very interested in old, worn-out items or, indeed, only military gear but anything that takes their fancy. They ended up with a pile of stuff including my water bottle (which I had put in a sock, discarding the army green cover) and one guy's brand-new boots. We first tried to argue, then tried to get them to pay, then asked them for a receipt, but they said "No". Paul called them a load of thieves and they agreed. They made him apologise, however, saying that he needn't bother coming back unless he did so.

We left Bol for Ndjamena, the capital. The whole town is shot to pieces. Every building is peppered with bullet holes. A burned-out tank lies halfway up the steps of the 'cathedral', the building itself gashed by bullet and shell holes. I actually like the town; it has a lively market and the locals are cheerful and friendly. Some enterprising souls even plaster up the holes in their houses – although it's only ever a matter of time before they have a rash of new ones. We heard that the airport was bombed only two weeks after we'd left.

We crossed the river to Koussiri in Cameroun and were soon struck by the contrast to Chad. It is lush, green and the people are unbelievably friendly and hospitable. I don't think I saw a single gun either and the police apparently don't wear them. We drove down through Mora, Maroua, Garaua. We've seen plenty of apes, usually crossing the road but they soon disappear as you stop. No elephants yet but they're here all right. The roads too in Cameroun are brand new, perfectly smooth tarmac as far as Ngoundere. After this it's good piste. The people live in humble mud and thatch hut villages nestling amongst the many trees and they all wave enthusiastically – sparkling eyes and teeth.

One night in Cameroun whilst camping, we heard singing and drumming so five of us waded through the cotton fields and undergrowth in the moonlight towards the sound. We joked about being just in time for dinner and finding ourselves on the menu! Instead we came across a procession of about twenty children, ages ranging from maybe five to fifteen. One boy had a drum, another was leading the songs and the rest were singing and dancing. It was absolutely fantastic and we danced off into the night with them eventually ending back at the truck where they sang and danced some more. It turned out that these were Christmas songs, very tribal and beautifully sung. We soon learnt the words and were able to sing along.

All too soon we arrived at Garoua Boulai to cross to Central African Republic. A very relaxed border crossing only cost two packets of cigs. The contrast is again striking – dense forest lines the road, the houses (now mud brick and rectangular) are spread along the roadside. President Bousaka moved everyone to the roadside during his regime. There is some hostility though from only a few, and virtually no agriculture – but no shortage of bananas! We drove through Bouar and went to Boali waterfalls 80km north-west of Bangui. Very impressive although plenty of French tourists. 3kms downstream is a rope bridge. It's nice and quiet here and we got a swim in the river and camped the night. One girl slipped on a rock and went for an unexpected dip with her passport and camera – losing her glasses as well – and what's more it was her birthday!

The group development is interesting and, predictably enough, not always smooth. It seems to have split in two; those who want to actually engage with Africa and those who don't. We also have a few lazy ones who let others do the work but it isn't that bad considering the length of time and the numbers. We've started having regular group meetings and this seems to be smoothing things out fairly well, although we do have one or two personality clashes.

We are now in Bangui. It's quite a pleasant town and easily the most western since Rabat in Morocco; there are even supermarkets. There is a strong French influence here and many of the larger businesses are French owned. This is supposedly an independent country but still relies on French money and troops to shore up the shaky economy and government. We're here until 27th December when we leave for Zaire. It is hot and sticky and not a bit like Christmas - hard to believe it's not midsummer back home. We've got Christmas dinner organised – a spit-roasted pig. Pigs roam the streets here, eating what they find like dogs in other towns. They're pretty timid though – with good reason I'm sure.

I'll close now. I have to go to collect our Zaire visas. I look forward to your next letter – don't worry too much. I'm having a great time. I wish you all a happy New Year, hoping all's well at home.

Love, Graham

PS   Oh yes, stomach upsets. I think we've all had or have diarrhoea – most of us feel okay apart from that, though one or two have been pretty bad. The food is excellent, varied and quite inventive - we even have an oven. The water is sterilised though occasionally green or muddy brown. Only one girl has had to take medication. For the rest of us it's no food and plenty of water for a day or two. If you'll excuse the subject – it is inevitably high on the list of conversation topics here!

Map 6a. The Zaire river basin.

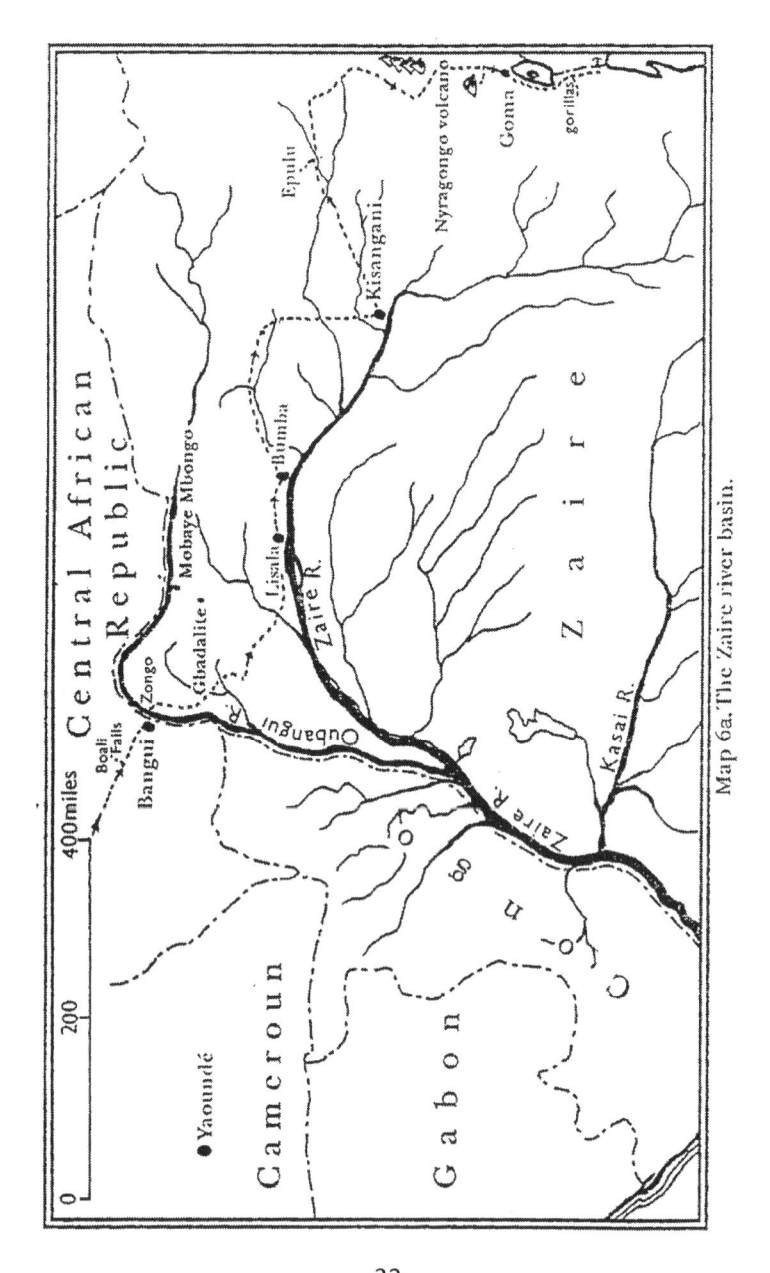

Received on 4th February 1986

Dear All,

I started writing a postcard but soon ran out of space so I thought a letter would be in order. I'd have written before but Zaire is a wild and unpredictable country with almost non-existent communications (making it the most fascinating country yet). If you sent mail to Goma I didn't get it, though we left a note for the following driver to pick any up. We left Bangui having had an enjoyable Christmas. Locals have three day drumming and dancing sessions.

I spent Christmas Day by myself walking around the small mud houses, almost every one of which seemed to be roasting a goat over a fire outside and having a party. I was invited to join very many. The churches were full of rousing cheerful singing and a colourful procession paraded with drums and dancing through the town to the mission where a Christmas service was held. Some boy scouts taught me dances and laughed at my efforts to play the tam tam!

Caught the ferry to Zongo, Zaire. It only runs when someone wants to cross so you first have to find the owner, then find the ferry, then give him diesel! The roads in Zaire are usually dreadful: potholed dirt tracks and in the wet they're ten times worse and there can be several trucks stuck in the same place for hours or even days. Everywhere we go children run enthusiastically to the roadside and wave wildly, though not only the children, for most adults smile and wave as well. Especially at this time – they all shout "Bon Année" and hold up gallon containers of hooch! We went to Lisala to try and get the passengers on to the river steamer (there was a TV documentary on it once – Great River Journeys). Everyone you ask gives different information, no-one really knows when it may turn up but it looked like being a two-week wait so we asked around the cargo boats and booked them all onto a barge carrying tar! We had four days of peace and quiet whilst they had a wet, hungry but very enjoyable time on the river. We drove round to Kisangani, breaking a rear spring in the process. Here we stayed in the grounds of a shabby hotel, well used by overlanders, meeting four other trucks though none from Exodus. Next we drove east to Epulu to visit the pygmies. A small group of us were lucky enough to go hunting with them (they are still almost entirely hunter-gatherers). It was really interesting though pretty gruesome at times. They are very cheerful people and for once I felt tall! They all have bows and arrows which they try and swap for clothes or trinkets.

We continued to Komanda, then south to Beni. Here the scenery changes from endless trees in a flat landscape to steep rounded hills with large banana plantations – pineapples grow wild. The 'road' twists and turns. Being the dry season we haven't seen too many mud holes and have only been held up by mud once – when we had to drive half in the ditch to get past another truck stuck on a hill and we found ourselves unable to get out. On that occasion there were altogether seven trucks stuck.

At the Equator we had an 'initiation Ceremony' which involved getting very wet. Up as far as Kayna-Bayonga the terrain becomes more mountainous as we mounted the escarpment before breaking through the pass to reveal the huge, spectacular Rift Valley. Now we were in the Virunga National Park and, after descending to the dry savannah of the valley floor we had a lion cross the road in front of us. We soon saw several more, plus hundreds of gazelles, warthogs and, later, a large herd of elephants. This was, for me, the highlight. It's quite an amazing sight to see elephants wild for the first time. We also saw large numbers of hippos in the rivers but, so far, no crocodiles!

Continuing now to Goma and Nyiragongo volcano. This last erupted in 1977 killing two-thousand people and, up till recently, had pools of bubbling lava in the crater. We climbed up to the rim (3740m.) in five hours – hard work but well worth it. The whole area is dotted with volcanoes. The crater is 500m deep and about 1000m across, sheer-sided with jets of steam and a strong sulphur smell coming from it. We stayed the night there in some small huts and came down next day.

We camped on the shores of Lake Kivu which, according to one travel guide, is warm and safe for bathing with no bilharzia, hippos or crocodiles. We subsequently discovered that it has more bilharzia than almost any other lake in Africa!

Now we're in Bukavu having travelled the beautiful mountain road and tomorrow we're going to visit the mountain gorillas. I'll leave a gap so that I can let you know we got back safely and anyway, won't post this until Burundi as it's so expensive and unreliable here.

Just got back from seeing the gorillas – wow! We split into two groups. We had four guys with machetes to hack a path through the jungle. After half an hour or so we saw the head of a large silverback male peeping over the bushes. We got to within ten feet of him – he was so placid – just sat there eating leaves. There were young ones hanging in the trees and females maybe twenty feet away. We spent about an hour with them.

Anyway, I'll close now as I've run out of room. I'll write again when I get the time and I'll try and ring from Nairobi.

Love Graham.

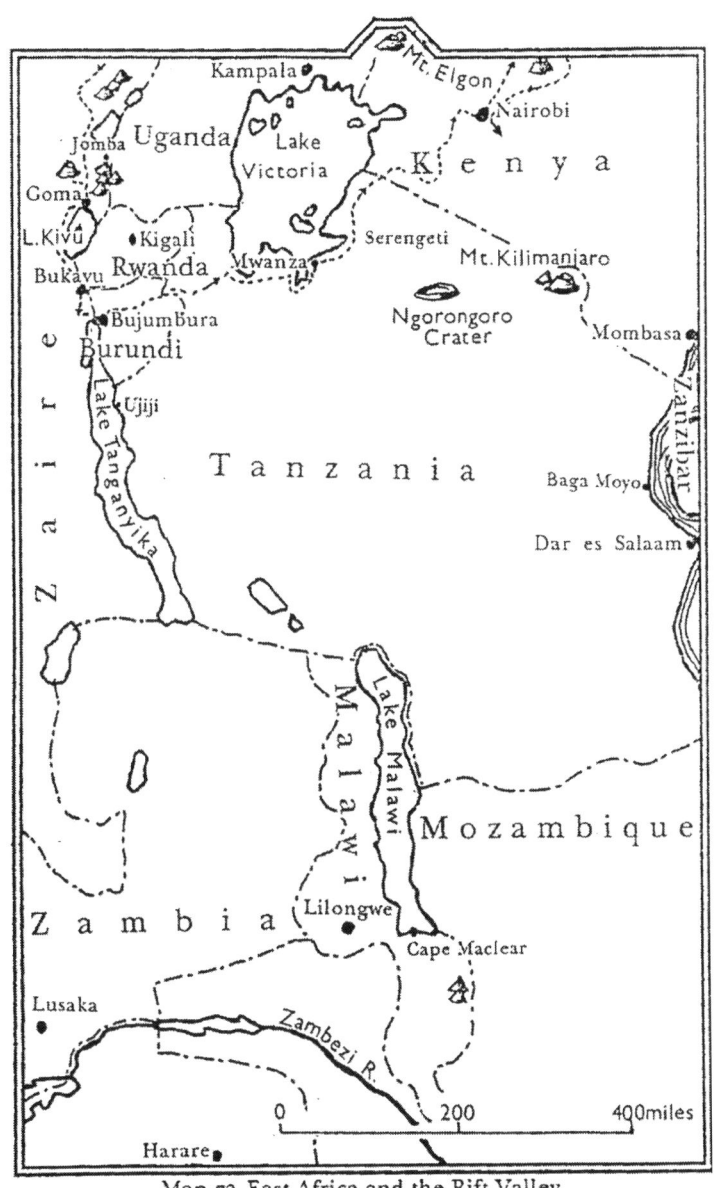

Map 7a. East Africa and the Rift Valley.

Received 24th February 1986
Kenya/Tanzanian Border.

Dear All,

I thought I'd write a short letter to keep you up to date on events.

After leaving Bukavu and the gorillas, we drove down the minor 'Kiliba' road because to drive down the main road to Bujumbura in Burundi means entering Rwanda for a short stretch. This would involve buying visas and also require multiple-entry visas for Zaire.

This minor road was a spectacular mountain track, very narrow and twisting. One hairpin bend after another, then we emerged onto a wide plain that led ultimately to Lake Tanganyika and the Burundi border. The borders are getting easier and we can now get away without bribing. We managed to spend our last Zaire money by buying beer off the police!

Soon we were in Bujumbura. What a contrast. Cars, advertising, garages, hotels, supermarkets. A culture shock. We soon had the now familiar crowd of souvenir sellers around the truck. I have hardly bought anything and don't want to load myself down with stuff. I am sorry to see so many of our passengers keen on buying ivory. I wouldn't touch it as we've heard all about poaching. (Incidentally we did hear about Dian Fossey's tragic murder in Rwanda by poachers).

Bujumbura is the capital of Burundi and we soon found that, like any capital city, it has its fair share of cheats and pickpockets. The two people shopping for the group's food that day lost about £20. Working in pairs, one guy 'accidentally' steps on your foot and tries to create a scene whilst the other picks your pocket. I heard their account whilst walking with them down the main street. Suddenly a guy stepped on my foot and started pointing to our feet and gabbling. I realised at once what was going on and grabbed the arm of the bloke who already had his fingers in my pocket. His mate ran off and I twisted the thief's arm so that I could see what he might have in his hand. Only a handkerchief to conceal the takings but he hadn't got anything of mine. He was pleading ignorance and looking scared. I told him to watch it and let him go, though some of the others seemed to think I should have punched him on the spot.

We camped on the shores of Lake Tanganyika which is like the sea, amongst the mosquitoes and even a few pelicans. It was just south of here that Livingstone and Stanley met. Most of the rest of Burundi is extremely poor and it is really only foreign money that has made Bujumbura fairly wealthy.

There's a brand new road most of the way through the country – though very little traffic to use it. We went by Kayanza and Muyinga to the border of Kobero. I've started collecting, as souvenirs, articles that people make out of rubbish, especially tyres and tin-cans (the people are very resourceful). Topographically Burundi reminds me of West Wales or sometimes Exmoor.

For some reason I'd expected that Tanzania would have good roads and all the trappings of Westernism. Perhaps it was that we're now driving on the left and the second language is English. How wrong I was. It's poorer and the roads are worse than Zaire. The towns are neglected and squalid and the people aren't always as friendly as we've been accustomed to. Perhaps this is partly a language problem as far fewer people here speak English as speak French in the ex-French colonies. The language here is Swahili and all I can say so far is "Hello" – a good start, but....

We drove past Biharamulo to Geita where the market square is adorned with the husks of two ex-Leyland buses. In a corrugated-iron cafe off the square I had already eaten half my red beans and chilli from my plastic bowl before finding the similarly coloured half-cockroach! And then onto the awful corrugated, potholed piste until we got to the ferry crossing at Busisi. There must have been fifteen other trucks there and we heard that the ferry had broken down two weeks before and would be out of action for at least a month. Two local guys offered to show us a way to drive around (not before asking for a fee), so we agreed. They said it would take three hours. It took twenty-seven! and involved getting completely stuck in soft clay which came over the top of the rear axle and took a lot of digging before we eventually got out after camping there the night.

The next day we soon got stuck again and almost recruited the help of a passing team of four oxen pulling a cart to get us out. But they were all going in different directions and kept escaping – it was quite a circus, so we persevered and eventually got into firm ground.

We spent the rest of the day in Mwanza, a fairly large town with a good market and cafes. It's even possible to buy chocolate and ice-cream! Now onwards round the southern shore of Lake Victoria towards the Serengeti. For a while now none of the overland companies have used Tanzanian game parks since they increased their prices by 700%. It's unfortunate, though likely, that we'll soon be using them again as some companies have recently relented.

We camped at a beautiful spot on flat grassland amongst towering granite tors, Rock Hyraxes (a sort of giant guinea pig), abounded on the rocks and we soon had dinner cooking. The moment we had finished eating it poured with rain and thundered for half-an-hour or more, flooding many of the tents. Not long after that, one by one, we went to bed. We've been getting up before sunrise since crossing the last time zone so I wasn't surprised when I was woken by my tent partner shaking me saying "Graham, get up". I sat up sleepily. "The whole area is crawling with ants", he said rather dramatically. I took the second statement to be a sort of 'by the way' but then I heard much chaos and confusion coming from the other tents so I asked if it was breakfast time or a midnight panic. He said that it was a midnight panic (in fact 1.30am). I was actually quite relieved to think that I had several hours of sleep left. The drama and screams escalated in the camp. So far we hadn't seen a single ant. He climbed out and soon he was hopping around "Ow, Ouch", slap, slap! Now he charged, blundering head-first into the tent, slapping his legs and tearing off his shirt. There were now quite a few ants in the tent but we put it down to what he had brought in and squashed all the ones we could find. I heard Geoff in the next tent taking it down and moving. "They're coming nearer" he said ominously.

I still hadn't accepted that I couldn't just forget it and go back to sleep.

"Do you think we'll get them here," I shouted, "There's hardly any here yet".

"Definitely" came the reply, "there's a huge line of them".

"Oh, well" I said, "I suppose we'd better pack out sleeping bags away before they are full of ants".

I pushed my sleeping bag into its bag and Peter did the same. It took only thirty seconds but when we shone the torch back at the door it was black and seething with ants. The hole at the bottom of the zip was like a gushing hosepipe of pins and needles. They flooded in like a black torrent onto the groundsheet.

"Time to leave" we agreed and Peter plunged out and hopped and screamed all the way to the truck some fifty yards away. I had to bang clumps of ants off the tent flaps with the torch as I would otherwise have collected a few hundred of them on the way out. I got to the truck, amazingly, without a single bite. There were eight people already there and more naked and semi-naked people were running comically with feet lifted high and shouting and swearing to the truck all the time. We soon swapped stories. Peter and I had been lucky indeed.

Paul was the first. He woke up with an itching at his head. Thinking it was probably mosquitoes, he turned on his torch to find, not only his pillow, his tent partner and his sleeping bag obscured by ants, but also himself. They soon danced, screaming and naked to the truck where water was poured over them to try and get the majority of the ants off. Whilst he was screaming, one large ant jumped onto his tongue and sunk in its mandibles! Four other passengers had similar experiences, the rest awoke before bring engulfed. Some people had to move their tents twice. I eventually went to sleep in the open safari seat of the truck and put up instead with enormous mosquitoes and swooping bats.

Next morning we could follow a very well-defined trail still thick with ants. Our box of rubbish was almost entirely hidden by the heaps of ants on it – forming bridges and tunnels with their bodies to get the food out. The victims' skin is creeping today though they are otherwise unharmed. What an exciting night... !

It's now the 2nd February and we've just left the Masai Mara game reserve where we spent the last two days. After the ant episode we took the road running parallel to the shores of Lake Victoria and crossed the border. This took quite a long time as they seem fairly disorganised, though friendly enough. On the very rough minor road towards Lolgorien we stopped for lunch and found that there was a small gold-mine 200m off the road. In all, four of us went down; the others neither not interested nor not keen on the idea of going underground. It was just like caving again. There were about fifteen men working the mine and they'd been at this one for six months. It is about thirty-five feet deep. Their equipment consists of three tin-cans made into oil lamps, one lump hammer, one large chisel and one bucket. They even gave us a nugget each when we left. Our geologist passenger says it's a very rich vein though probably not very extensive.

We were in the Masai Mara game reserve at first light next day, having camped just outside. As I crawled out of my tent at dawn I was greeted by the sight of a giraffe picking at an acacia tree in these African plains beneath the wide African skies. As we set off after our open air breakfast we soon saw a large herd of water buffalo, and later lions and wart-hogs. By the river we stopped to see about 30 hippos in the water, just their eyes and nostrils protruding; they are huge when they come out. Later we stopped at Keekorok lodge, a luxurious place built for tourists. The management does not exactly welcome grimy and stingy overlanders but the staff are very helpful. I got thrown out of the gents' toilet for washing but the security guard showed me a shower that I could use instead. There are hot-air balloon rides over the park each day and five of our group decided to go the next morning. It costs $250 (American) for one hour's fight followed by a champagne breakfast and a Land Rover safari. Very expensive but I would have loved to have gone.

Next morning as the balloonists left in a Land Rover we went in search of wildlife in the truck, especially elephants. One of our group is an artist who specialises in painting African game and is crazy about elephants. He'd brought his easel and a half-finished painting so he could get some photos to prove to his customers that he'd really been to Africa. Soon we spotted a herd and drove up to it. They were amongst trees by a stream and we walked up so close that one bull charged. The three of us watching them ran the couple of hundred yards to the truck in fear of our lives and all tried to get in the cab at the same time! We found twenty giraffes in a group with several young ones. Gazelles, zebras, wart-hogs and wildebeests were everywhere and you tend to ignore them after a while.

We'd had a good peaceful time when we decided to follow one of the tourist safari buses that run from the lodges, thinking that he may know some good spots. He did! We followed him down a narrow track to where there were already seven other minibuses. They were watching a pride of lions basking in the sun. One by one more and more of these minibuses, plus several Land Rovers, turned up, all facing in different directions on this narrow track on a fairly steep slope. At the peak of confusion there were eighteen vehicles, including our own. In trying to pull out of the way, one minibus had got really stuck so all the miserable passengers had to climb out and push. The lions, fifty feet away in the bottom of the valley, didn't move but did look bewildered at all this chaos. Being right behind the floundering tourists we decided we ought to lend a hand to their pathetic efforts. When all the blokes from the truck jumped down the lions decided they'd had enough and ran away, though not before one of them let out a mighty roar, sending half of us clambering back in.

Later in the morning we left Paul at the lodge, so he could get the accounts up to date (Alan, one of the Exodus managers, is going to be in Nairobi) and I took the rest out looking for more elephants. We spotted a large herd and eventually got within fifty feet or so of them. Our artist has primarily come on this trip to get a photograph of himself standing in the savannah with his easel up and elephants in the background. We got some good shots of just that, though I wasn't very happy about him walking too near them.

The balloonists had a great time and felt that it had been money well spent, though were sorry to have missed our adventures. We're now camped just outside the park on our way to Nairobi. We should be there on Wednesday 4th February and I'll send this and try and phone from there.

Well, that about wraps it up for the moment. I've come to the end of my list of things to mention. Thanks very much for your long letter, Mum. No, I didn't breathe a sigh of relief at the end and very much enjoy getting letters to read – the longer the better! I haven't had a chance to re-read it yet to see what else I should let you know so I'll leave this letter open until Nairobi – so much for being a short letter!

It's now the 6th February and I've left Paul in Nairobi with Alan, the Workshop Manager. I am taking the passengers around the Kenyan game parks. Kenya is so English it's unbelievable; fish and chips and all. Nairobi is a great city, not too big but clean and friendly. English is spoken usually as a first language. We'll be back there on the 12th and leaving on the 14th and 15th. It turns out I am going all the way to Johannesburg after all and I'm pleased to be able to see the group's progress to the end.

Relationships within the group have reached a new level. People generally have come to accept each other's differences and are getting along quite well at the moment.

After hearing that my letters are being typed and handed out I'm aware that I'll have to write more of general interest. The only problem is that it's easy to recount horror stories with relish and I'm sure they're entertaining but, although true and unexaggerated, do tend to give a false impression, and put other people off travelling. Rest assured that I never take risks but also try not to miss opportunities.

We have had all-night watches and fires in case of wild-life straying into the camp. Most animals, however, even lions, will not come near to such a large human presence. Elephants sometimes will but we are constantly told that they'll do no harm. Anyway, I haven't had an elephant in my tent yet!

We are now in the Meru National Park, north-east of Nairobi. We saw a lot of elephants on the first evening and some stood in the road in front of us. Despite trumpeting and stamping their feet, our big, white elephant is obviously considered a match and they soon walked away. There were plenty of noises around the camp that night. It is a designated site but there is no fence or anything. Nearby live five large white rhinos. They are the only ones left in Kenya, possibly in the whole of East Africa, as they have been ruthlessly poached. Unlike their black counterparts they are very placid. In the mornings they graze in the campsite. We were able to walk right up to them and to even touch them. I'd have felt more nervous in a field with lively cows or a bull. The guard was concerned only that we didn't stand too near their horns as I suppose one toss of the head could be a nasty surprise for someone with their back turned!

This park is the one in which Elsa, the lioness in 'Born Free' lived. I instantly recognised a rock outcrop called Leopard Rock as the one in the final scene of the film where Elsa has her own family. There are some waterfalls now known as Adamson Falls after Joy Adamson, that we also went to. During our lunch in a beautiful glade by the river, we saw our first crocodile. It didn't move for an hour. We could only see its eyes and nostrils above the water. I'm sure it wondered whatever was going on.

There are virtually no tourists in this park, a welcome change from the Masai Mara. We saw only one other Land Rover all day. We'd met the English occupants at the campsite the previous night and they were travelling in the opposite direction. They told us that the road ahead had been washed away and suggested we follow their tracks on a diversion through the bush. We had to drive right through tall bushes with four-inch thorns continuously for about 4kms. I did wonder if we'd get out at one point but we really had to as I certainly didn't want to walk 30kms through this place to find help! Anyway we're back at the campsite and off to Nakuru at 6.00am to see the flamingos.

It took almost a day and a half to get to Nakuru as they're still making the road and it is really dreadful at the moment. The flamingos and pelicans are impressive; huge pink and white patches on the lake and an occasional cloud of swirling pink and black. We've had a really easy two days here – spending the night at Makalia Falls campsite. There would normally have been a beautiful cascading waterfall and shady pool but there's no water. No matter, there was a shower and a toilet. Of course there were no other people here unless you count the hundreds of baboons that live in the rocks. We've seen a lot of baboons over the last few weeks. They roam around like stray dogs and are usually harmless if you ignore them. One thing never to do is feed them as they can then get very aggressive.

Tonight they didn't really bother me; there was no moon and I figured that they wouldn't be stupid enough to go rock climbing in the dark. Anyway, they are daytime creatures. We clustered the tents closely and went to bed. Soon I was fast asleep. I awoke, it was hot and I was sweating. I lay awake and alert as I could hear movements amongst the tents. Then, in chorus, the deep gruff bark of the baboons came first from the rocks where they lived and then from all around us. Each time the chorus would last for maybe twenty seconds and end with one baboon making a different noise to the rest: sort of ... Ugh, Ugh, Ugh, Ugh, HAH! Then would follow a gap of several minutes before it would start again. It was as if they were chanting and I hoped that it didn't concern us. I found it very difficult to get back to sleep again; it was very eerie, the noises echoing round the cliffs. My tent partner, woke up as well. "What's the time?" I asked, expecting to be after 4.00am. "1.00am", he said, so I had another five hours of this! I considered how I might defend myself with a tent pole should a ferocious baboon burst in through the door but I did eventually get to sleep and was glad to awaken, unharmed, to the comforting daylight.

Well, this really has turned into a bit of a marathon letter! I'm safely back in Nairobi now and the passengers have said that they've been pleased with my leadership over the last week, which is good to know.

I'm going to finish this letter once and for all now. So until the next one, keep warm, don't worry.

    Love
    Graham.

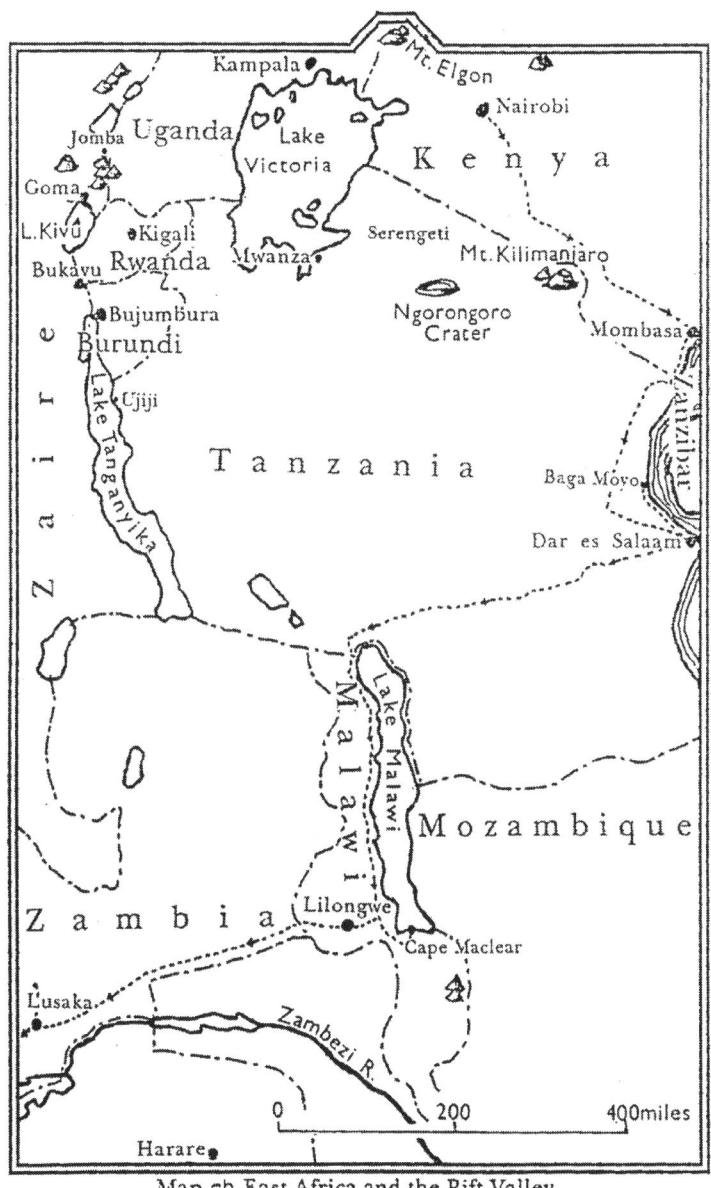

Map 7b. East Africa and the Rift Valley.

Tanga, Tanzania,
22nd February 1986

Dear All,

These letters seemed to have assumed the role of a diary as I haven't had time to keep one *and* write *and* keep up to date with my log.

We left Diani Beach today and also Kenya. We've all enjoyed the rest. The first full day I walked for five or six hours along the dazzling white beach. It's good to be alone sometimes and also surprising the difference in attitude of the people I meet. It's useful to have a pair of dirty, patched shorts and car-tyre sandals. No-one tried to sell me anything or ask anything of me but, instead, chatted genuinely with me. The next day, after shopping, myself and Kjell, our Swedish passenger, hired snorkelling equipment and entered the weird world of fish, sea slugs and coral. There is a coral reef off-shore and there are some beautiful starfish and enormous sea cucumbers plus various colourful fish. The sea is body temperature so you can stay in more or less indefinitely. In the afternoon I hired a bicycle and went off alone to explore the area. The coast is rather touristy, all the hotels' clientele are white and mainly German. We have been in a small campsite outside a hotel and have been free to use their facilities though they're very off-hand with campers – rooms in the hotel being £50 a night.

In five minutes I was well and truly back in Africa having left the tarmac road for the network of narrow paths. These paths run between the coconut groves and banana groves, between mud huts and people working. Before very long a young man of about my age started asking where I was from and where I was going. We walked and talked for a while until we came to the village where he lived. He introduced me to some of his friends and bought me a cup of something like chilli tea! It was refreshing though spicy. He then took me into a small building with walls that were open from waist level. Here an old woman was cooking. It was the village 'Cafe'. He spoke to her in Swahili and we sat on one of the benches. An old tin full of water was brought and this was for washing our hands. A bowl of cassava root cooked in coconut oil was produced, along with a mug of rice porridge. It was really good, the cassava root is like sweet potato and we've probably seen more of this growing than anything else throughout Africa.

Next I was taken to the chief's house. He was sitting under a tree eating cashew nuts. He spoke no English but my friend translated. He bade me welcome and was interested to know how I came to be there. After this I was introduced to a man who was building a house which was, for me, fascinating. He was using coconut leaves for the roof. Now I was taken back to the home of my guide to meet his wife and little girl. They live in a small clearing, overshadowed by huge oak-like trees, in a mud and wattle hut. These huts are really only used for sleeping in as the people actually spend most of their time outside. Again I was fed; his wife provided maize meal and lumps of chewy meat in gravy (which, as a vegetarian, I ate to be polite). Next stop was the nearby village where four local schools were having a volleyball competition. All primary colours and smiles; the school uniforms throughout Africa are always bright and simple, far better, I think, than the drab conventional uniforms in England. We went to another small cafe where Alex, my guide, met some more of his friends and they bought me tea and a bun before I was wished 'good luck' with much hand-shaking and was on my way back to the camp.

It's now the 22nd February and we are just north of Dar es Salaam in Tanzania. We've just met another Exodus truck and both of us went on a day trip to a place called Baga Moya. It was originally Bwaga Moya and this meant 'lay down your heart' probably because it is so beautiful here in the sun amongst the palm trees that you'd never want to leave. The name was corrupted, however, to its present Baga Moya which means 'crush the heart' because this was the terminus of the slave caravans that had come from the interior, usually Ujiji, on Lake Tanganyika. Baga Moya was the harbour from which they would be shipped to Zanzibar just across the water for sale to Indians, Arabs or local growers. Here it was that their last hope of seeing home again died.

We went to the 'slaves' house', now the police station, where the thousands of slaves would be crammed into small dark cells awaiting shipment. On the long journey from Lake Tanganyika they would be made to carry huge tusks of ivory for which demand was growing. Women slaves with babies would watch their babies killed so they could be made to carry more. People who fell sick on the way would be killed straight away to deter others from feigning sickness in order to escape. Over half of them would die on the way.

Many missionaries may have been misguided, ill-informed or caused more harm than good but, the ones who came here did much good. As many as 50% of the bidders in the Zanzibar slave market would often be missionaries, funded by begging letters sent to the rich philanthropists of the developed world. At Baga Moya they founded a 'freedom village' for the slaves they bought to set free. David Livingstone spent some time here as he was very concerned at the plight of the slaves. It was at Ujiji that Stanley finally met him, the place that slaves would be first held until there were enough to make a caravan.

It was by a ruined mosque behind the mangrove swamp that we first met 'Professor' Kejeri. He was to be our guide and, for the job, he carried a twelve-bore shotgun all day. No-one knew why, and he had earlier said that cartridges were hard to find so I doubt it was loaded. He was an interesting guide; if you gave him a photograph of yourself he'd write your address in a book and you'd get a number: 'Friend number 4546'. We watched the dug-out fishing boats unload their fish on to the beach where they were immediately auctioned. Being shallow here, the sea was actually hot. I got chatting to a man in the market who said he was the skipper of a large fishing boat. He commented that I was changing my colour and said that he'd lived in Norway for four years during which time he had been surprised to find that he'd turned paler.

It's now the 2nd March and we're camped on the shores of Lake Malawi, the second largest lake in Africa after Lake Victoria. Driving through Tanzania again, the poverty is ever more apparent. The country is completely broke and foreign currency is in great demand. We have to pay the frequent road tolls in US dollars whilst, for other things, T-shirts are more valuable than Tanzanian shillings. If it were not for the black market exchange rate, which is twelve times better than the bank rate, it would be ridiculously expensive. As it is, though, it works out fairly cheap. We drove the good road from Morogoro to Mbeya.

Rain is becoming more frequent as we are about to enter the rainy season in this part of Africa. Also, sometime in the last few days we've passed the zenith of the sun. That is, as we're going south and the sun's going north, we have crossed paths, the sun being directly overhead around midday. From now on it will be in the northern sky.

From Mbeya we drove south through Tukuyu to the Malawi border. Having got three copies of *Africa on a Shoestring* on board, we had read its warning: that the book is banned in Malawi and likely to be confiscated at the border. As a guide it is usually out of date and often inaccurate. It is nevertheless invaluable. In its commentary on Malawi, in the first edition, it had said some uncomplimentary things about Banda's dictatorial regime.

Before we got to the Malawi border, however, we had to get out of Tanzania and this involved a complete truck and pocket search, plus much paperwork and money counting. Now, with *Africa on a Shoestring* stuffed into various sleeping bags, we approached the Malawi border post. It's a good job we did have copies, though, as otherwise we wouldn't have known that women *must* have skirts or dresses extending to below the knee, bell-bottom trousers are banned and men must have short hair. (Banda had been a doctor in Edinburgh during the sixties). I had mine cut the night before in preparation. Also any nude pictures whatsoever are banned. We had the most thorough search yet during which they found one of the books. On to the immigration control and I was picked out as needing a haircut! (One of the others on the truck stuffed his under a hat and got away with it). One of the girls had to hack away at the nice haircut she'd taken half-an-hour over the previous night. This done we proceeded into Malawi and were instantly struck by the friendliness of the people. One of the criticisms in the banned book was that there was too little money put into education, public welfare, medicines, etc., and too much into new road building schemes and ambitious western-style projects. If that was the case in 1982 it doesn't seem the way now. Indeed the education here seems amongst the best we've seen.

I wasn't too happy with 'His Excellency; the Life President' Dr Hastings Banda, on arrival but as somebody said "A good dictatorship is better than a bad democracy". He seems to have done his country well despite his Victorian attitudes. These attitudes seem, though, to have a double standard. It is quite usual to see bare breasted women in town or naked men bathing in the rivers, and even in the capital Lilongwe, on the bridge over the river, is a sign that reads: 'NUDE BATHING IS FORBIDDEN – WITHIN SIGHT OF THE BRIDGE'. As with many of the countries we've visited, photography is also forbidden.

For the last two days we've travelled down the side of the lake amongst fields and hillsides covered with sugar-cane, peanuts, cassava, tobacco, bananas and rubber plantations. It's fairly mountainous here, again, like Burundi, reminiscent of Wales. It's Sunday and as in all areas of Africa it's easy to tell as everyone is dressed in immaculately clean clothes of glowing colours. Sometimes the women carry parasols / umbrellas and it all looks uncommonly 'civilised'! I've not yet had a chance to go to one of the lively Church services but we did get a peek in through the door of one as it was just warming up; drums, bright colours, big smiles and everyone enthusiastically singing and dancing. If Churches were like that at home there'd be no keeping me away!

We're now camped well off the beaten track, again by the lakeside. As usual we soon had a crowd of people, mainly children, watching, fascinated, as the tents went up; tables came out, fire lit and music played from the cab cassette player. Down on the beach several fishermen sat talking around their dug-out boats, having already laid out their fish to dry.

I took the opportunity of sitting quietly alone in the sand, hearing nothing but the waves. Some of the others had decided to have a wash in the lake further down the beach. I'd been there for thirty minutes or so when something in the water just off-shore caught my eye. A large buoyant mass. I looked again and it was gone. I scanned the waves until sure I had been mistaken. As I stood up to leave, however, the huge pink head of a hippopotamus rose from the dark water. It turned to face me and yawned enormously. I quickly told the others that swimming was not a good idea by which time many people – children, fishermen and our passengers had crowded on the beach near this monster. It would disappear for two or three minutes before rearing its head once more to watch its amassed spectators. Judging by the stir it caused, it was obviously an unusual event and when it yawned again the children cheered and clapped. Apparently pleased at the response, it obliged again before finally sinking from view and moving quickly away.

It is the African people themselves that are really the central and most interesting object of our journey.

Having now travelled through eleven African countries I feel that I've been to some degree able to compare and contrast the various races and cultures. There are some striking exceptions to the often similar ways of life and thinking. Perhaps the most notable is the Masai in Kenya and Northern Tanzania. They are tall, slender people with straight noble features. They are really the only people who still universally wear traditional clothes. They are a very proud people and do not allow themselves to be photographed without substantial reward (we heard of one overland driver who sneaked a photo and found a spear under his chin until he paid up). They grow no crops at all and prefer huge herds of scrawny cattle to small herds of good cattle, as it is the number of cows that is their measurement of wealth and social standing. Also the Masai are one of the few peoples who aren't interested in our old bottles, tin cans or T-shirts.

In the Central African Republic the people, and especially the children, were always after reward. All the time we saw begging hands, and strong words if they received nothing. In Zaire perhaps more than anywhere else, we had to be very careful with security.

It is important to remember that we are seen as people of unlimited resources and, as such, fair game and all too often easy targets due to slack security. It's very difficult to keep an eye on everything though – in the dark with sometimes hundreds of children and youths standing all around the campsite, just watching or trying to sell souvenirs.

We learnt our lesson but it took the loss of a bag containing a passport and other important valuable travel documents, a blanket and some clothes, (which were actually returned) and two shovels. Every time such theft has occurred it could have been avoided through our not presenting irresistible opportunities.

Surprisingly Tanzania isn't so bad, despite the poverty, though there are plenty of requests for gifts from children. In Kenya and Malawi there's virtually none. The children wave without holding out cupped hands and usually want no more than addresses. Incidentally, if letters start arriving from sundry Africans please reply to them – or perhaps some of the children at school would like to – as they are mostly young teenagers that I've given your address to (sometimes it doesn't work telling them that my address is the truck).

One thing that has throughout been remarkable is how rarely I've seen children cry and I've never yet heard one whine or complain. Children from about the age of five have the newest arrival tied on their backs. The babies don't mind at all and the children seem to take very good care of them. From this age also they have to do a share of the work. After walking they must learn to carry things on their heads. In fact, *everything* is carried on the head. I saw one little boy in Niger walking alongside his mother carrying on his head a small packet of washing powder and I've often seen little girls carrying anything from a single tin mug to huge bunches of bananas in the same way. School children en masse in many countries spend a certain amount of time each week in the fields. With so much work to be done and so many children per household no doubt parents don't have time for whining, though I've not yet heard anyone shout at or seen anyone strike a child.

In eastern Zaire especially, loads are carried on the back on a strap that is supported by the forehead. In this way bigger loads can be carried. Old women carry sacks of charcoal twice their size or large bundles of sugar cane fifteen feet long. Ten year old children – often with a child on their shoulders as well, carry five-gallon water containers this way.

The men rarely seem to carry anything, though are not entirely lazy. They do the building work, much of the work in the fields and often look after the children. The women certainly do the bulk of the work, though, and are the real masters of the household. There have been times in the markets where one of the men from the truck has carried the shopping for one of the women and caused quite a stir amongst the locals who consider it a woman's duty to do all the heavy work. As long as they accept their roles the system will work. I think that the western industrialised nations have reached the point where the sexes no longer accept their former roles.

People generally get married at between fourteen and sixteen years of age and usually have large families. There is a high infant mortality in most of Africa so I suppose it balances out. The men usually outlive the women who not uncommonly die in childbirth (or perhaps from exhaustion). The average life expectancy is around forty-five years and it is rare to see anyone that I would consider old. It's fairly difficult for people to marry outside their own tribe and they must first seek permission from the community leaders. The tribal heritage is still strong but I think that it's now being seen in the light of national unity. This has been perhaps Africa's greatest problem, that the political boundaries imposed by European counties took no account of the very complex existing societies and their own various boundaries.

In the towns there are always several people with treadle-powered Singer sewing machines out on the street. They seem to have enough work despite there sometimes being ten or fifteen of them side by side and I've had several items of clothing made by such people. Also you'll always find street shoe-repairers. They sit on the pavement surrounded by broken and worn-out shoes, cut up truck tyres, hammers and nails. I've seen several using broken crankshafts for lasts. In Mwanza was a group of young boys almost engulfed, on the street, by old tin cans, light bulbs, etc. They had a small charcoal burner with six or seven home-made soldering irons heating up on it. Out of the cans they were making oil lamps, funnels and ladles. Elsewhere I've seen oil cans, watering cans and shower roses, sieves, drums and rattles made from old tin cans, not to mention the ingenious toys that boys make for themselves. Old tyres become sandals, buckets, corners for crates and boxes, and handles for tools. Inner tubes are cut into long strips and are used everywhere in place of rope or bungie cords for tying down loads on bicycles or hand-carts. In the Sahara they were made into water carriers for lifting water out of wells. The rim rubber, also found in truck tyres, is used for resoling shoes. Truck wheels throughout Zaire are hung from wooden frames to become church bells. Old bicycle rims are used by children as hoops. Oil drums, large and small, can be covered with skin to become a drum or made into a charcoal stove or opened out to become doors, gates, roofing or road signs and cut out and hammered into shape as woks or washing tubs. Old plastic sheets screwed up and bound tightly with twine are the only footballs available to the vast majority of young boys.

Whilst in Malawi, we spent two nights at Cape Maclear just 18kms north of Monkey Bay on the southern shores of Lake Malawi. What a beautiful place. All around are steep rocky wooded hills rising out of the clear blue water, itself an aquarium of the most colourful fish. Across the water the dark rugged mountains of western Malawi are silhouetted. It was while sitting in a rock looking out at this wild scenery that I had one of the rare moments of realising just where I am. It's so easy to take it all for granted and to allow my mind to be completely occupied with the day to day routine, the needs of the truck and, of course, the passengers. It is, after all, my job and, I might add, the most demanding and rewarding job I've had. I enjoy dealing with the group, I enjoy the responsibility and look forward to the day that I run my own trip, but these moments of solitude are important to me to put it all back into its grand perspective.

We are now regularly getting spectacular thunderstorms each evening, exhilarating in their ferocity. Most of the two days we spent at Cape Maclear Paul and I worked on the truck, doing the backlog of small jobs that had built up while the others lounged around in the sun. From here we returned to Salima and then over the mountains to the capital, the new capital, Lilongwe. If I'd have woken up and found myself in Milton Keynes I wouldn't have been at all surprised. This town is virtually identical; the same numbered areas, meaningless to a stranger, the same long dual-carriageway avenues flanked by sterile parkland. The solitary and dispersed public buildings, the roundabouts, the same impracticability of getting around without a car. The same age and, who knows, the same planners! It's just as inhuman and hard to find your way around, though aesthetically it is very green and pleasing. It's a show-piece diplomatic city and of little interest to us. We passed into Zambia with no problems. We'd heard some bad stories about the police, military and border officials here but, so far, politeness is rewarded with helpfulness. Anyway, nobody has been arrested yet.

They tend to have rather silly road-blocks: one, a veterinary road-block, was only interested in scrounging medicine from us. Another 'Tsetse Fly' control barrier had a guy with a can of fly spray who squirted a bit here and there, and carried what looked like a large butterfly net!

Near the border with Zimbabwe is a bridge that is guarded day and night by the army with tripod-mounted machine guns at either end. It has a speed limit of 5kms per hour and apparently they get very upset if you exceed it. The white Zambian farmer we're staying with tonight told us stories about having his farm surrounded by guerrillas during the last war around 1980 but he says that it's peaceful here now. We're off to the Victoria Falls tomorrow, and at this time of the year, the water is high. Should be good!

Since Nairobi we've lost three passengers and gained two that were originally on the other truck that left England the same time as us. The American girl who left us is on her way to London. That should be a shock to her system as she's swapped all her clothes for souvenirs and she's never experienced London in February! Our Canadian has caught another truck going north via the Middle East on the second leg of his journey to Kathmandu. The other Englishman has also flown back to London.

The group is now fairly stable though, of course, it is nearing the end of the trip so some of them are gritting their teeth. Decisions are now, thankfully, usually unanimous which makes things a lot easier. I've voluntarily joined the cooking roster to get a better idea of how it feels and am presently trying to puzzle out a more comprehensive rota system to include all the necessary jobs together.

I still have no idea what I'll be doing when I reach Johannesburg. I'll try and phone anyway. All the way through Africa we've not been able to say where we are going to anyone. Up to Kenya we were going to Nairobi. Afterwards, Lusaka: and now it's Victoria Falls. Botswana is reasonably friendly towards South Africa so there's no problem there. Most of black Africa will have nothing to do with South Africa and stamps in your passport will mean being refused entry into many countries, especially Zambia and Tanzania. South African nationals can hardly travel anywhere in Africa. I still intend to enter South Africa with an open mind but the nearer I get and the more I read, the more my mind is made up. I'm not taking sides but trying to look at it realistically. Anyway, I just hope that I'm there long enough to have a look around and get a balanced view. I'll write my impressions in my next letter but, until then, I must sign off.

Love
Graham.

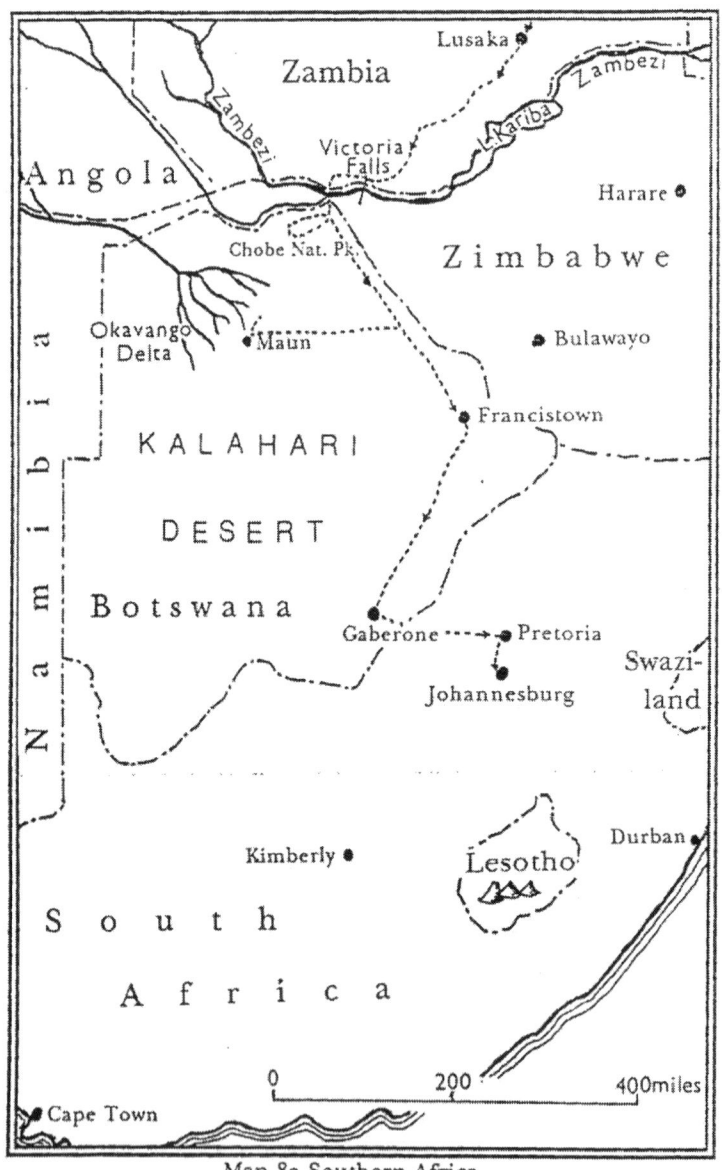

Map 8a. Southern Africa.

14th March 1986, Maun, Botswana

Dear All

We're having a couple of days off here at the Okavango River Lodge at the edge of the Okavango Delta. This is a rather unusual geographical feature as this large river never reaches the sea but instead empties into the Kalahari Desert, forming huge swamps that evaporate in the heat. We had hoped to be able to take a speed-boat in and, after a couple of days, a light aircraft out, but at the moment there's not enough water for boats. It's very expensive to just fly in and out for such a short time, though some of our people have done this. Others have gone on an hour's aerial sightseeing so it seemed like a good opportunity to put pen to paper.

After leaving Lusaka, from where I sent my last letter, we drove down the good road to Livingstone – 'the tourist capital of Zambia'. It's a bit of a one-horse-town, 7km from Victoria Falls. Considering its grand title and its proximity to one of the Seven Wonders of the World, you'd expect to be able to at least buy a postcard - but no such luck. It's possible to buy postcards of the Swiss Alps or of log cabins in Scandinavian pine forests but 'Victoria Falls'? Nope! It is almost as if it is deliberate policy not to advertise this, Zambia's second most valuable asset after copper.

Anyway we camped in the campsite near the top of the Falls. We'd been able to see the rising cloud of spray from well before Livingstone (it is said that in the right conditions it's visible for 50km). One by one we walked down to the Falls and that first sight is one that no-one who has seen it is ever likely to forget. Here it is that the mighty Zambezi River, over a mile wide at this point, plunges three-hundred feet into a narrow chasm before churning down a narrow twisting gorge cut deep into the basalt. The vastness is overwhelming as the thundering cascades are shrouded in every plane by clouds of spray, so that at first its depth can only be guessed and its width only wondered at.

The Zambezi forms the border between Zimbabwe and Zambia and the greater part of the Falls is in Zimbabwe so next day we all walked across the bridge after completing customs and immigration formalities for our day trip to Zimbabwe. Here they've exploited the tourist potential rather more than in Zambia; there are a couple of very grand colonial hotels where we were able to get a good meal.

I walked the full width of the Falls on the opposite side of the precipice. It's necessary to wrap cameras etc., in plastic bags and wear either raincoats or have a change of clothes. In two minutes I would not have been wetter if I'd jumped in the river. It's not a fine mist but torrential downpours that pour upwards from the gorge. After lunch five of us lashed out $20(US) for a twenty minute flight around the Falls and up the Zambezi. The afternoon storms were approaching fast as we raced down the runway. Soon enough the landscape quickly expanded, revealing the horizontal treescape and several dark marauding storms stomping menacingly from north to south. We banked hard and wheeled round to face the spraycloud. The sun still shone as we made our first right-handed circuit.

Photography was difficult as it was as bumpy as the truck up there. At one point the pilot flew straight towards the waterfall banking vertically as we cleared the top so that all I could see out of my window was the immense churning splendour of the chasm. I grabbed my camera, hurriedly wound it on and fumbled to find the viewfinder before the awful spectacle was lost for ever; but all was dark and it was lost forever as I found myself looking down into the lens holding the camera upside down! We circled four times and could easily see at least five earlier sites of the Falls as they had to cut back through the basalt plateau. Now we flew up the calm waters above the Falls; a steamer lazily chugged on its way as we descended almost to river level to fly past before soaring high to see a group of hippos clustered like bacteria in a green culture. Now the trees flicked past beneath us as we made a wide circle to avoid a towering thunderstorm and soon were looking down the runway. We touched down without a bump and no sooner had we climbed out of the aircraft than the storm caught up and great globular raindrops smacked against the windscreen of the minibus taking us back to the hotel. It had certainly been money well spent.

The next morning we left and headed towards the Botswanan border, an hour's drive away to the west. We've been camping with another Exodus truck; Mick and Dave's group, who are due to finish on the same day that we are. They were somewhat behind us when we arrived at the Zambian exit post and ferry. The ferry is a crude barge capable of carrying two trucks. Not many years ago it was bombed by the Rhodesian army and was out of action for a long time.

Safely across, we walked into the Botswana Customs and Immigration office; passports were duly stamped, forms completed before we were asked for our 'Botswana Road Permit'. We did not know these were necessary but were under the impression that we could get one in Francistown, 500km further on. It was true that trucks had previously been let through to do this but the officer said that "this was just a favour". He was obviously fed up with all these tourist trucks constantly turning up without permits and expecting favours. He decided to draw the line in front of Q88 VAM. He decided we must go back to Zambia and apply for a permit from Lusaka; this, he said, could take three months! We couldn't go back to Zambia anyway as our Dutch passengers need visas and their previous ones were only single entry. To bypass Botswana and drive through Zimbabwe is, we were warned, inadvisable due to the political situation. (It was after ignoring such advice, a few years ago, that the 'Encounter Overland' passengers met their unfortunate and well publicised end at the hands of guerrillas; though the driver and women were released). It appeared we were stumped. We argued, we reasoned, we pleaded for an hour and a half, dreading that at any moment Mick and Dave's truck would come trundling round the corner expecting more 'favours'. Eventually he agreed to let the truck in as far as the 'Chobe National Park' whilst Paul hitch-hiked the 500km to Francistown, picked up a permit and returned. To make sure he did, they kept our 'carnet de passage' which is worth more than the truck! Soon after, the other truck turned up and went through the whole thing again with the same result. Dave and Paul went off to Francistown while Mick and I spent a day and a half in the game park. The countryside is beautiful, blue weed-covered rivers, short trees and open grassland – but apart from a couple of crocodiles and a few elephants we saw little game. Still, never mind, we have now seen so much we are getting a little blasé about it!

Paul and Dave returned, having spent a whole night and day in moving trucks, tired and without permits. They did, however, have a letter from the Chief Commissioner, ordering the border post the let us and all future tourist trucks in as far as Francistown.

So now we drove flat out (45 mph) down the brand new asphalt road to Nata, in convoy with the other truck. It being my birthday we decided to have a party so stocked up with beer before turning right towards Maun on the good, but dusty, piste. The landscape is fast becoming desert. Vegetation is more sparse and palm trees were silhouetted against the sky as we stopped for the night.

Rain threatened so we erected both our cook-tents; the large awnings that fasten to the side of the trucks, in such a way that they joined together to make one large tent. After dinner the liveliest party for ages started with games and then dancing which kept going until 2.00am (very late indeed by our standards). Certainly a birthday to remember.

Whilst in Francistown, Paul had telexed London and received information as to what I'm doing after we reach Johannesburg. It looks like I'll be flying immediately to Nairobi to be co-driver to Kelvin down the same route back to Johannesburg. It seems that Kelvin's trainee, Ben, has given up. I'll know more when I arrive so I'll phone up then and send a mailing list as soon as I can.

Love
Graham.

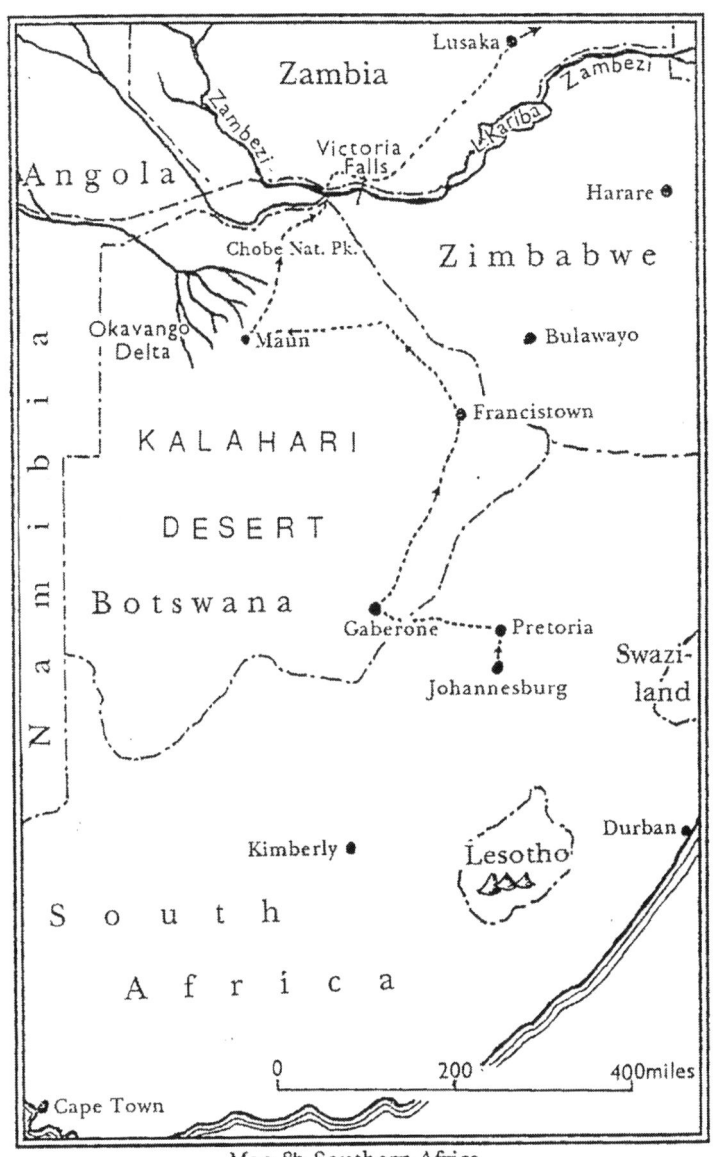

Map 8b. Southern Africa.

Victoria Falls, 8th April 1986

Dear All

It seems like a long time since I last wrote and a lot has happened in between. Where do I start?

South Africa. Six days was not nearly long enough to look around but it was long enough to get a glimpse of the beautiful scenery here and a chance to talk with South Africans of various colours which is really what I wanted to do. The first thing that struck me was the huge number of windpumps that are spread across the landscape. They're nearly all in working order unlike the ones in Britain.

The first night we spent in South Africa was at the municipal campsite in Rustenburg. There is a large sign at the gate that, somewhat arrogantly spat 'Whites only' at us. Up to then my first impression had been black and white living side by side. We'd stopped at a couple of towns and met friendliness and cheerfulness from the inhabitants, though the whites seemed a little suspicious of us. This sign gave the place a bad taste. The campsite was, as might be expected, provided with services undreamed of for some time. Hot baths, showers, a swimming pool with spiralling tubular slide, flush toilets, etc., etc. All this was maintained and cleaned by an army of blacks. For some time I found it hard to look people in the eye; the blacks because I was allowed this 'privilege' denied to them through no other virtue than the colour I was born, and the whites because I could not in any way bring myself to agree with the system they're maintaining and often defending.

Anyway, it being the last night of the southbound trip, we all packed our bags in preparation for our arrival in Johannesburg.

The roads are good, though reputedly have the worst accident rate in the world. Soon we were slipping past palatial mansions with security guards, tennis courts, swimming pools surrounded by barbed wire and tall hedges. Johannesburg is an affluent city, though the polarisation between rich and poor as well as black and white is sharply focused. We stopped in a gated car park at the Chelsea Hotel in the Hillbrow area, notorious as the 'wrong side of town'. The hotel is, however, comfortable enough, and the management and staff friendly and tolerant to the mess that rebuilding trucks in their car park can bring. The other Exodus truck was here, so after phoning home and going out for an excellent Chinese meal with the group, we went to the disco that was in the basement of the hotel.

One of the passengers from the other truck is a white South African and I spent some time talking with her. She said that over the years much has changed here. Apartheid is being relaxed in many areas (there are now some mixed race buses, probably introduced because the black buses are packed and the white ones empty). I don't like to sound cynical and I don't doubt that progress is being made but it seems painfully slow and all too often insincere. Public toilets are separated into 'Whites only' and 'Blacks, coloured and Asian'. The system may change but the attitude of the whites, especially the Afrikaans, seems unlikely to do so. They are not about to give up or share all their wealth and high living to people they genuinely believe to be inferior. The South African girl agreed that things are not likely to change fast enough to prevent social upheaval sometime in the future.

Whilst working on the truck several black people approached me individually to chat. One old man told me that he could be sent to prison for talking politics with me – though every conversation with either blacks or whites quickly spins around to the subject. The mood of the young blacks is one of despair and many are quite willing to take up arms in the struggle. It seems that there are at least four camps; the radical blacks – we read their pamphlets in Tanzania and it's very powerful revolutionary stuff, not likely to be good for anyone in South Africa if they should succeed. Then there is the moderate black camp, seeking to work for political change within the system but seen as helping it by radicals and therefore targets for their terror. The moderate whites, traditionally the English speakers, are seeking to dismantle apartheid whilst the hard-liners – rightwingers – resist every move in that direction. It does seem, however, that the more change is held back the more violent will be the eventual and inevitable change. Whites are arming themselves to the teeth. There's a gun shop not far from the hotel that is doing a roaring trade in hand guns. The shop was always full.

Their attitude is usually defensive and their friendliness and hospitality is often followed by such statement as "Now you can tell people in England that the streets are not littered with bodies" or "It's a really nice place to live; we have everything we want here; it's just the black ones ..." They are very eager to reverse the world media opinion of themselves.

Enough of politics ...

There followed that night a very confused and thoroughly unpleasant episode. On our south-bound trip there was an Australian couple, our geologist, Geoff and his partner, Ailsa. Ailsa was very loud and often got drunk. She's had a turbulent life and had many problems. Geoff was quiet, well-educated and had become a good friend to me over the last few months.

After our Chinese meal, during which I had talked with Geoff at length about our impressions of South Africa, we returned to the hotel. He went to bed and Ailsa joined the rest of us at the disco which was open to anyone. She was soon drunk and intent on pouring out her troubles as she always did. I had listened often to her stories and was in no mood for it tonight. The disco was good fun but eventually our people drifted back to their rooms. Having had limited success at holding the attention of any of the group who knew her only too well, Ailsa had taken to talking to two burly white men at the bar. At around this time I went to bed myself.

I was woken in the morning by Paul, who told me that Geoff had been attacked in his room. He was alive, despite having been stabbed seventeen times in the chest and back. It seems that Ailsa had brought one of the men from the disco into the Hotel and told the security guards that he was her husband. She'd announced her room number but they'd both soon gone back to the disco. Sometime later, whilst she was slumped over the bar, the man had returned to the hotel, had no problem with security as he had already been recognised, had gone up to the room on the third floor, opened the unlocked door and attacked Geoff. He'd then left the hotel and was not seen again. Geoff had managed to crawl to the room next door to raise the alarm and get an ambulance. It seemed the most likely motive was money. They weren't short, but nothing had been taken – perhaps he'd been disturbed – I don't know. I went to the hospital and Geoff will be out in a week having suffered a punctured lung. Not the best place to say 'Goodbye' to a good friend after having travelled together for four and a half months.

Over the four days at the hotel our old group gradually dispersed and our new group arrived. I was generally too busy working on the truck to notice who was who. We're taking back the truck that came down just ahead of us. Theoretically it has had a lot of work done on it. In reality it's hard to see anything that has been done.

On the 25th March at 10.50am we left Johannesburg. It was good to get away from the city again, despite a loud clacking noise in the engine and a bad oil leak. We crossed back to Botswana and headed back to the Okavango Delta. All the way the roads are good but we managed to find no fewer than twenty-two faults with the truck in three days. We sent our passengers into the swamps for a few days. They left on a plane and we got ourselves oily. We decided to try the short-cut road from Maun to Kasane. The truck was still throwing a lot of oil (four litres a day) and still clacking, but we made it. The road was sandy and muddy in places, a long way from help and in a large game park, but we only got stuck once in two days.

So, once again, here we are at the Victoria Falls. Having got a few days here we removed the cylinder head. One holed piston and smashed rings, the broken pieces of which had welded themselves to the top of the piston causing it to hit the valves. The nearest Bedford dealer is in Lusaka, almost 500km away and that's if they've got the right parts. Otherwise it means waiting four days or so for parts to be flown here from the U.K. To get us to Lusaka we removed the damaged No 1 piston, con-rod, cam followers and push rods and put a piece of inner tube and a jubilee clip around the big end journal. It took most of the day but it ran, albeit very roughly, on five cylinders.

The day before, at the local hotel, we'd seen a poster advertising 'White-Water Rafting on the Zambezi'. The company is called Sobek and we'd met their Victoria Falls operations manager in Mombasa in February. So we went to their office, a small chalet behind the hotel, and introduced ourselves. Charlie Ross, a tall, bearded American, told us that, at the moment it wasn't possible to run a trip as he was going away for a few days and he didn't have enough guides. It's not the most popular season.

"Oh dear, what a shame," I thought with relief.

Paul was rather more disappointed, having done canoeing in the Himalayas, especially as Overland drivers get a free trip whilst passengers pay $150 US for the day. Early the next day we went to town to get some money changed in the bank. There was a tap on my shoulder and who should be behind me but Charlie. It turned out that he didn't now have to go away and he could run a trip for us on Sunday after all.

After asking the group, almost everybody wanted to go (*they* hadn't seen the photographs in the Sobek office!). Did you see that BBC documentary on one of the Great River Journeys of the World where they went down raging rapids in rubber dinghies? I'm afraid I did and the thought of being effectively flushed down the toilet left me cold. But when I'm supposed to set an example and offered a free trip in the hope that I'll persuade future groups to do it, I was left with little choice. All day the feeling of impending doom lingered. Listening to one of the world's largest waterfalls on one of the world's highest flow-rate rivers almost at its annual peak and imagining the violence of all that water squeezed into a gorge sometimes only thirty feet wide. I searched for an honourable way out but there was none.

All too soon Sunday morning came around and, suitably dressed in light shoes, shorts and T-shirts we filed silently, like the condemned to the wall at sunrise, to the hotel. The hotel bus had been hired for the 10km drive to the starting point. With the amount of water in the river at the moment it would apparently be too dangerous to start at the falls as they do at lower water. Charlie was cheerful, despite having a bad toe, and did his best to put us all at ease.

Soon we met the Land Rover that had broken down with all the equipment and the boats, so this was all loaded into the bus too. It was a very steep walk down into the gorge. The Zambian guides and porters made light work of carrying everything down and by the time we got to the river, they had almost inflated one of the boats.

Behind this scene of practiced preparation was the awful backdrop of monstrous whirlpools, erupting surges, brown murk. My stomach churned almost as horribly as the river, though 'river' fails to describe this thing now before me. Was I really about to be launched into the jaws of *that*?

Charlie gave us a reassuring safety talk about what he wanted us to do and the many ways we would be rescued should any of us fall in – and not to worry if we did as this could be "quite fun". There were two boats, one for Charlie and the group, all with paddles and sitting astride the tubes, and one for the three Zambian guides and non-paying passengers, *i.e.* Paul and I.

So, hearts pounding, we pushed off. Our boat had only one oarsman, there mainly to orientate the boat rather than propel it. He often had to struggle against the rushing torrent which sometimes goes upstream as furiously as down; such is the mad confusion of the water. After the first small rapids I found myself enjoying myself! I'd had a sneaking suspicion that I might enjoy it as I've felt similar apprehension before and seen it dissolve into enjoyment. Caving was probably the most obvious but cycling in Europe and coming to Africa also. After an hour and a half we stopped at a beautiful spot for lunch. There's a small waterfall here that cascades down the sheer rock face into the gorge; it falls into a deep pool that we all plunged into for a bathe. The gorge is spectacular and made all the better by knowing that this is the only way anyone ever gets to see it. Everyone's fears had vanished as we ate our lunch of sandwiches and fruit juice.

Eagerly now, we climbed back into the boats but before we set off once more, Charlie stood up and seriously announced that just around the corner were the four biggest rapids of the day, following each other almost continuously. He said that there were some huge waves and that this was the most likely spot to capsize (though again he assured us that this also could be fun). So it was nervously once again that we pushed off to the mercy of the mighty Zambezi.

On flat water, marked by swirling currents, we floated around the sharp bend in the gorge. Ahead, the water looked flat enough but a second glance revealed that it had a horizon and ended abruptly. The nearer we came, the more of the chaos beyond came into view. I found myself chewing at my lip in anticipation. Over the smooth rounded edge we slid into the pit of a deep trough. All round us was towering, exploding water. It was my and Paul's job to throw our weight onto the bow as we rose out of the trough and hit the massive standing waves to prevent us being flipped over backwards. Even so, at times, the boat was almost vertical as I held on to the rope with white knuckles. Several times waves crashed completely over us, taking me by surprise more than once. Each wave seemed to drive us backwards as we smashed into them but, in a moment, would give way to another, often rising up right before us or to our left or right. As we came out of this first rapid I looked over my shoulder; one of our crew was out and one of our passengers from the other boat was also out, both detached and being swept helplessly down. Several more of the passengers were in the water but had managed to hang onto the rope. After the rapid, the river once again flattened out as it rounded another sharp bend. Both boat-crews were now rowing with all their strength to get within rope-throwing distance of the 'swimmers' (as they are euphemistically called) before the next set of awesome, wild rapids that was irresistibly advancing upon us. The swimmers looked quite unperturbed, probably because they couldn't see what was coming up, being so low in the water. Again we threw the rope but it tangled, short. "Swim" we shouted under our breath. But swimming was useless in the current. I saw the bow anchor line and started to uncoil it. One of the crew helped me as it was so tightly bound.

Again I glanced ahead. Another ten or fifteen seconds ... Two of the crew were untying the rear anchor line. We threw the first and the Zambian crew member grabbed it. The rear one was then thrown for Phillipe, our floundering Frenchman. It missed! Now almost over the edge. The rope hurriedly gathered up, thrown again. In range but the rope is sinking.

"Grab the rope". "It's right there". "In front of you". "Hurry". "Yeah". He found it and was quickly hauled in as had been the Zambian. They both slumped gasping in the bottom of the boat, exhausted and shaken but, thankfully, safe. The oarsman struggled to orientate the boat in order to hit the waves end on and ...

"Here we go again!" "Yeehaa!"

Going over these enormous rapids on an inflatable is great fun but I must say that I wouldn't like to do it in nothing but a rather thin buoyancy aid.

After a total of about 15kms and three hours on the water we landed at a white sand beach and made the long, steep climb out of the gorge. It felt so good, not only to have done it but to have faced my fear of it. (I don't think I shall be doing it every weekend, though).

Charlie wasn't too happy about the trip. It was the second consecutive trip where people had fallen out on the same rapid. The waves, he said, were bigger than he's seen before on this stretch and, in future, he was going to seriously consider having a couple of oarsmen to manoeuvre the boat so that the passengers could sit inside, which is far safer but involves less participation for the passengers.

Today, Monday 7th April, we were all set to leave for Lusaka. Bump-start – flat batteries and off to Livingstone for shopping. Our five-cylinder engine, badly out of balance, feels horrible. Livingstone has also run out of diesel and we have barely enough to get to Choma where there is a depot. Suddenly – shudder, shudder – CLANK, CLANK. So we're back at Victoria Falls campsite. We've stripped the engine down again and Paul's hitch-hiked to Lusaka in search of parts. It's all highly entertaining – I'm told that I will most likely be flying back to UK from Nairobi for a break before bringing out a southbound trip as leader. So I might see you soon!

Love, Graham.

Victoria Falls, 18th April 1986.

Dear All

I'm writing this on our fifteenth day at Victoria Falls. I think I told you about our engine trouble in the last letter. Paul went to Lusaka almost two weeks ago to try and buy the necessary parts from the Bedford dealer there. Meanwhile I stripped the rest of the engine and the passengers sat round the swimming pool. Stewart, the other co-driver, had incurred the wrath of Mr Gillespie in the London office, presumably because he was responsible for overhauling the truck in Jo'burg. After a couple of days I received a Telex from Paul through the Sobek office. It read:-
"Parts not available here so being shipped out on Saturday. Stewart to find his way here by Saturday to catch flight Monday. All the best, Paul."

No-one was too surprised either about the parts or about Stewart being sent home. Anyway, there's plenty to do around here, even if it's just sitting by the pool and catching up on letters and cards. We expected Paul to arrive on Sunday evening or Monday. I rebuilt both front hubs. Monday lunch time I received another Telex:-
"Stewart on his way. Plane cancelled so parts not arrived. They are due to arrive late 15.4.86. P. Mallinson on way with mail and letter. Hope to be with you Wed.pm/Thur.am
Regards, Paul"
This was greeted with a still good humoured "Oh, no".

We were rapidly exhausting the possibilities of Victoria Falls. There were, at one point, five overland trucks in the campsite so we had a couple of parties and got to know each other. I also helped one driver remove and replace his gearbox and Kelvin, another Exodus driver, change one of his springs. The mysterious 'P. Mallinson' arrived with the mail from Lusaka and this raised morale greatly. It turned out that his brother, Dave, works for Exodus and is presently in South America; he, on the other hand, is hitch-hiking through Africa alone and had stayed at the same place as Paul in Lusaka. He also brought a letter from Paul saying that the parts had got as far as Rome and that if any of the passengers wanted to head off alone and meet us later, they were, of course, welcome to do so.

Perhaps it's because they're a fresh group, perhaps it's because they know that it's neither Paul's nor my fault, but none of them have complained. It is unfortunate though, as several of them are only booked on the six week Johannesburg to Nairobi section. The group, fifteen in number, a nice sized crowd, includes ten women and five men, plus Paul and I. A little unbalanced, and just a little bitchy from one or two quarters! We have eight Australians, five British, two Canadian, one Frenchman and one Austrian. Their occupations include an aircraft engineer, estate agent, town planner, nurse, farmer, cartographer (and even a mechanic!).

Thursday 17th April came around as quickly as days go by sitting in the sunshine drinking cold beer or coke. Paul did not arrive that morning, even though I had prepared everything so that we could get straight on with it and I cut short my early morning visit to the impressive Livingstone Museum. At around midday, as we had joked, another Telex arrived:-
"Parts in Johannesburg but airline left documents in Rome. Will now arrive 18.4.86, I hope.

All the best, Paul"

We had to laugh! But, laughing apart, this proved to be the last straw for most of the group. They found out 'probable' train times to Lusaka and left at 2.00am on Friday morning intending to hitchhike from there to Malawi where we will meet them. Three Australian women are keeping me company and it's now quiet, relaxed and peaceful in the camp. Only the mischievous little vervet monkeys to keep an eye on as they creep up and snatch food even from the pans on the fire.

Thanks for your letter, as always a pleasure to receive and to read once I've managed to sneak away from the questioning and chores of the group. You say that it must be strange to leave one group, having lived closely with them for five months and to take on a new lot. It didn't feel strange – in fact it felt good. Not because I'd had enough of them but because this was, for them, the end of the road. The goal they had worked, and at times, longed for. There was no more for them to do. It was good also to hear them say how much they had got out of the trip and how memorable it had been. From the group I received a beautiful book and, from one girl, £15. For them it was a sad parting but for me a meeting of new passengers in which the excitement offset the sadness. The only time a tear crept into my eye or a lump into my throat was saying "Farewell" to my good friend in hospital – about whom I wrote in my last letter.

Yes, but ...

I'm sorry but it has to be said. You say in your letter that we, in our civilisation, which has taken thousands of years to evolve into its present form, cannot be compared to the natives of Africa. Of course, I will not deny that this is largely true; over the past centuries European culture has learnt much about social and industrial development, especially since the industrial revolution. Before this, despite many other differences, Europe then, as Africa today, was a continent composed primarily of subsistence farmers.

Part of Europe's rapid expansion during the industrial revolution included colonising the 'primitive' continent of Africa, without its people's consent or, often, understanding. Africa was a continent without nations but with strong tribal boundaries. These were ignored by the European colonists who carved up Africa with straight lines and without concern for its population. From that time until today each country has followed different lines according to the attitude of its previous European administrators.

For some European colonists it was considered important to begin to teach the principles of government to the African people, for whom the concept of national identity was entirely new. Tribal boundaries are still strong today, though they are leading to less conflict than they did, perhaps because of the efforts of national governments to instil a sense of national identity. Other colonists chose to keep the Africans in ignorance and run the countries themselves. For all of them, things happened faster than they would have liked.

For some colonies, notably the French and British, where Africans had been allowed to develop at least some experience of government, independence, though perhaps a little premature, was arranged amicably. Trade and economic links were maintained from which each partner benefitted. The Belgian Congo, however, where Africans had been largely excluded from government, was dropped by Belgium like a hot potato when it demanded independence, to sink into years of bloody tribal conflict and many short-lived governments. In other countries, some of the more stubborn colonists who refused to accept the demands for independence, were eventually overthrown by the African majority. All of the independent African countries suffered a drop in their standard of living and government, some very much more than others. But those countries where western principles of government had been taught and implemented, slowly gained experience and stand some chance of ultimately returning to something like their former prosperity. They also have often been fooled and tricked by unscrupulous western businesses into buying unsuitable technology, products or projects.

This brings me to South Africa. It can be argued that the 15% white population are no longer 'colonists' but have now assumed the status of having a birth-right to live in the country. The Rhodesians also thought this and also said that they would never succumb to African rule. The world knows only too well of the growing demand for black rule in South Africa; history suggests that they will get it, and probably soon. The white South Africans are afraid of this but their resistance tends only to increase the violence. Tribal divisions are exploited, and inflamed where possible by the government, in order to prevent black unity which would certainly spell its own downfall. Black rule now would very likely bring turmoil and chaos to South Africa – Africans having been completely excluded from positions of authority. It is true that education for the African population is one of the best in the continent, but education in government has been completely and deliberately absent. The Asian and 'coloured' population has succeeded in gaining a nominal representation within the administration but the huge majority of the population has none.

Today is the sixth Anniversary of the independence of Zimbabwe. We regularly listen to Zimbabwe radio. It's interesting to note that this radio station is run along BBC lines. It has little advertising and relies on licence fees for its revenue. Apart from that, it plays, I consider, very good music. The new African government has retained much of what the colonists left behind. I believe we have a lot to learn from each other and do not arrogantly believe that we have all the answers. We undoubtedly have many in the field of industrialisation etc., but Africans have a resourcefulness, cheerfulness and instinctive love of life, not to mention community spirit, that we in the west could learn much from (this is what I meant when I referred to the churches – they've got *soul!*). I don't dislike my own culture or, by travelling, shun it, but hope to understand it better by seeing how different places have developed under different conditions.

So much for the essay ...
So you want to hear about spiders, snakes and other creepy crawlies, do you?

On the southbound trip we saw only two or three snakes all the way. There are plenty of lizards but these dart away; then again, so do the snakes. I've always been told to walk heavily in likely snake country so that the snakes can feel you coming (they can't hear) and get out of the way. They don't want to tangle with a human as they are rather more likely to be killed than we are. On this trip, though, we saw a 'puff-adder' in Chobe National Park. It slithered over Stewart's foot. Stewart, it must be said, is a keen snake enthusiast. He has a snake-catching stick and old fang scars on his arms from a long-ago encounter. This snake was probably about five feet long. Puff adders are responsible for 80% of snake bites in Africa and can easily be fatal. Like most snakes, however, they prefer to avoid confrontation. This particular one would have too, if it hadn't happened to slither over, of all people, Stewart's foot. It was soon pinned to the ground by the stick across its neck and, after we'd all been given a thorough guided tour, it was killed. Stewart was loathe to kill it but said that they have regular routes and it would likely be back before morning. No-one fancied having it as a tent mate so … Actually the passengers who had been into the Okavango Delta recounted that they had stepped right over one on a path and had all stood over it to look at it – this snake that can throw 40% of its body off the ground and strike a man in the throat. They know better now!

On one of my day trips to Zimbabwe I visited a small snake park. Behind a curio shop is an array of glass cases and walled pens. Soon there appeared, slinking in through the doorway, the owner. A short African man with thick black hair, a long moustache and small pointed beard, his eyes staring in the secure knowledge of what a snake bite can do. In slow deliberate musical tones he guided us round his precious snakes. It's hard at first to take him seriously as he callously sing-songs his expert way around and also difficult to avoid being hypnotised by his mesmeric 'snake' eyes and rhythmic, soothing voice. He picked up his favourite pet, a ten foot black mamba, telling us that it was one of the most deadly snakes in the world, whilst a small tortoise persistently tried to climb up inside his trouser leg. After seeing his stone-still crocodiles, five legged frogs in alcohol and dried snake venom, we left as though under a spell, feeling it had all been rather a strange experience.

As for spiders, we've seen few of note though there are some very colourful ones. The largest one I've seen was bright green. Its body was shaped like a shield and was perhaps an inch-and-a-half long. Far more prevalent are cockroaches, often four inches long, which regularly infest showers and toilets. As I write, there is a large praying mantis on the table in front of me. They're harmless enough but can give you a nip if annoyed. There are some enormous grasshoppers and beetles but these are never a problem, more often a curiosity. Sometimes, though rarely, we see scorpions, usually whilst collecting firewood. We are constantly aware of the presence of snakes, scorpions, etc., but there's no point in letting it bother you. Just don't pick up stones without first kicking them over to see what's underneath or walk through long grass in bare feet (even though the locals do).

Love,
Graham.

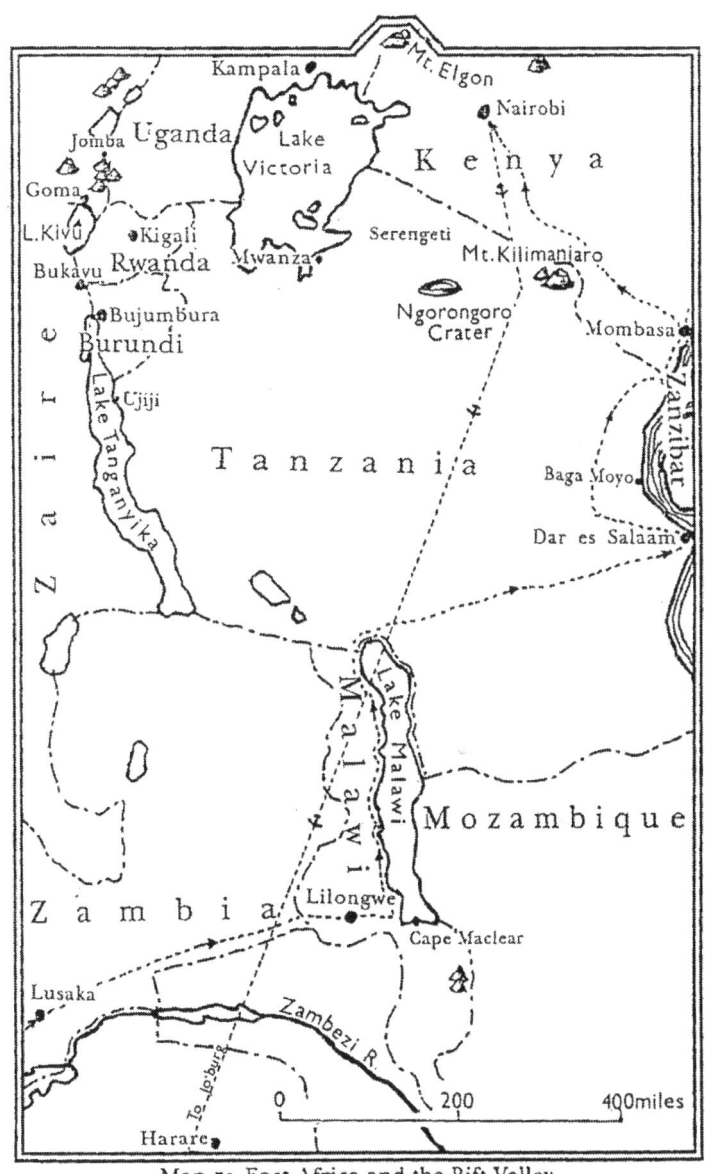

Map 7c. East Africa and the Rift Valley.

Map 8c. Southern Africa.

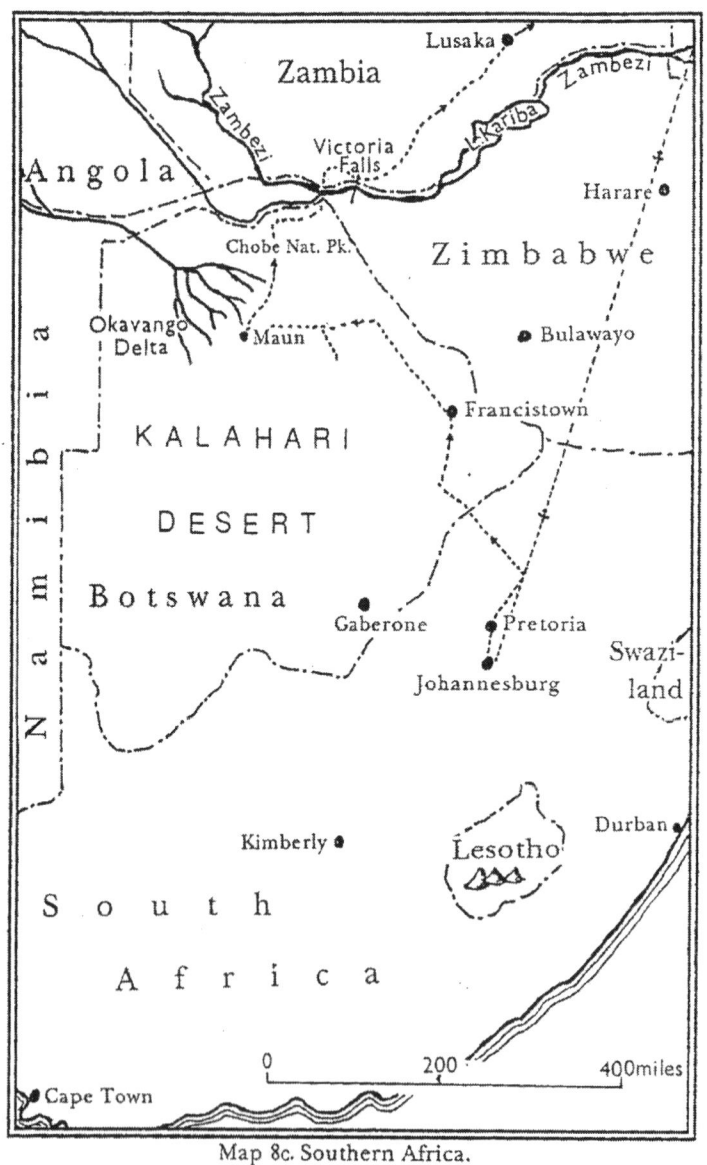

Island Safari Lodge, Maun, Botswana. 25th May 1986

Dear All

Okay, I know I haven't written for ages. I've been really busy. After eventually leaving Victoria Falls three weeks, two days and five Telexes late, Paul pushed the group very hard indeed. I actually didn't agree with this at all, especially since it was now largely *my* group as he'd been away for so long. Leaving three weeks late from the Falls and arriving only four days late in Nairobi I felt that those on the six week Jo'burg/Nairobi section had got a raw deal and I'm sure it wasn't Exodus's idea (although they did all get an offer of a free trip later).

I arrived in Nairobi on the Saturday at 6.00pm and was presented, as expected, with an airline ticket by Paul who'd come on a few days ahead of us. "Aren't you going to look at it?" he urged. I was a little puzzled by his eagerness – after all, we had both known for weeks that I was to fly back to London. I opened it. But what's this? Johannesburg?! My flight was at 7.00am the next morning. It had been decided that I would run a northbound as leader as soon as I'd got the vehicle ready.

I was understandably sorry to leave the group that I had got along with so well. Also I was disappointed at not coming home for a while as the previous plan had suggested. But I was glad to get the chance of running a trip myself and felt completely ready for it. The group was to be a very manageable size of nine and I wouldn't have a trainee to worry about until Nairobi, by which time I should have got well into the swing of things.

That night we had a big celebration and farewell party at a restaurant and disco followed by talking and drinking until about

4.00am. My flight was at 7.00am so I knew it wasn't worth going to bed as I had to be at the airport at 6.00am and it's an hour's drive. Soon after it was light I boarded the British Airways 747 and was pleased to find that I had a window seat forward of the wing. The harsh runway soon faded away and the dull, overcast Kenyan sky became a dynamic three-dimensional dream. Soon we were breaking through into a sunny world of billowing snowy mountains like somewhere over the rainbow.

"If the plane were to plummet now," I thought, "how could this fantasy landscape harm us?"

After a short while the captain announced that we were to make a slight detour in order to get a view of Mount Kilimanjaro as it was well above the clouds. We flew by about level with the top; its enormous size was given away by the length of time I could see it from the window of this aeroplane zapping along at several hundred miles per hour. What a sight! Rearing conical, hard, dark and solid from the dreamy, fluffy topography around and topped with the white blood of clouds it had pierced. I wondered how many people were standing on the top watching us, having slogged for four days in thin air with constant nausea, headaches and no sleep and me eating my plastic breakfast sitting in a warm armchair, sorry I'd left my camera in my baggage.

Somewhere over Tanzania the clouds disappeared and the earth below looked indistinct and often uninteresting - the sky above, a deep, orbital blue.

Before long we were gliding low over the flashy houses, swimming pools and tennis courts of suburban Jo'burg.

Back then to the Chelsea Hotel in Hillbrow. For the next week Kelvin, one of Exodus's longest-serving drivers, and I rushed around Johannesburg getting jobs done, paperwork sorted, necessary shopping, etc. In the evenings I'd go round to Kelvin's apartment which he shares with Nikki, his girlfriend, for dinner as it's far nicer than the hotel. Visiting so many places of work was also an eye-opener. The one constant criticism of black workers is that they're lazy and won't do anything unless you kick them. This is true. They work in slow motion and do as little as they can get away with. But if I were to be called a 'black bastard' or only ever shouted at, talked down to and never trusted to do anything other than the lowliest menial work – and paid less than my white colleagues – then I'd also work in slow motion and do as little as I could get away with. It's a vicious circle and I don't see any way out of it.

So on the 20th May I left Jo'burg on my first complete leader trip with nine passengers to Nairobi – and who knows after that. They're a good bunch, lively and much more 'arty' than the previous groups, which suits me fine. Four of them can play the guitar so I've bought another (my first one fell apart). We've had singing and dancing in the evenings fairly regularly. They're also much more keen to meet African people than the other groups and, being a small group, we don't tend to swamp small communities as twenty people often do.

Six weeks from Jo'burg to Nairobi is easy and relaxed so I've been visiting all the places that Paul drove past and have been spending days here and there. Being leader is much more demanding than being co-driver but the rewards easily outweigh the extra burden. I feel in control, I can now easily answer questions I'm asked and, most importantly, I can run the trip my way. Of course, time will tell, but I aim to do this job well.

Today we entered Malawi, probably my favourite African country for which, again, I've had my hair cut. It feels good to know where I'm going and to know the best places to take people and also to try out new places.

Rosie at the rock engravings in Zambia

Victoria Falls was again enjoyable and we spent five days there this time. I've got quite a few friends around there now! Charlie from 'Sobek' rafting company ran a 'world-first' highest-volume white-water raft trip for my group with the Zambezi in full flood but, unfortunately, I had to provide transport to and from so couldn't go, though I did get some good photos of people falling in on the first rapid!

No doubt you heard of the bombings in Harare, Gaberone and Lusaka by the South African military on the 19th May. I diverted to miss Gaberone but obviously couldn't miss Lusaka. We stay on a farm 15km out of town, run by an expatriate ex-vicar. He'd heard the bombing and told us that it wasn't the ANC at all but a UN refugee camp that they'd hit, killing two and injuring eight people who were visiting. Whatever next?

We're now back in Kenya having spent two weeks in Malawi and ten days in Tanzania. This truck doesn't seem to like Tanzania. We'd wrecked a water pump in northern Malawi; then on the Malawi/Tanzania border we completed the tricky border formalities to the sound of our right rear tyre deflating. At Bagamoyo I had to change a spring. From there I took the back road to join the main road north to Tanga. After 10kms of dreadful track out of Bagamoyo there was a small ferry to cross a river – that day the scene of much activity. Men were busy welding, hammering and sawing. I was soon approached by a large well-dressed man who was obviously in charge.

"This ferry is closed," he said to me.

It looked usable to me and I didn't want to drive the 200kms alternative so I tried debate, argument, pleading and bribery to no avail. He was, he said, in charge only of servicing the ferry and not running it. During the time it took, however, the ferry made three crossings carrying bicycles, mopeds and Land Rovers.

"If the ferry is closed" I argued, "how come it's made these crossings?"

"I'm just helping these people," he said.

"Well, why can't you help us?" I asked.

"Your car is too heavy" he replied, "you'll have to drive back to Bagamoyo and find the district engineer and ask him to give you a letter saying that you can cross, then there will be no problem".

This may sound fair and reasonable were it not for the appalling road with stretches of axle-deep creamy mud and huge holes, not to mention our chances of finding the district engineer or of persuading him to give us a letter if we did. I had no intention of driving back. I decided to sit it out and try to reason with the man until he got sick of the sight of us.

I found locals who told the boss they'd seen similar trucks use the ferry before but he wouldn't budge. He did become more friendly though and gave me chunks of his sugarcane to chew. Eventually I conceded that there really wasn't an alternative and I'd have to drive back and try to find the district engineer. I climbed into the back of the truck where some of the group were preparing lunch.

"Okay." I sighed, "we're going to have to go back to Bagamoyo".

At that very moment a Land Rover appeared with three men inside. I had a sort of feeling that it may just possibly be...

"This is the district engineer," the maintenance boss said rather proudly. He asked him in Swahili whether we could use the ferry to which he apparently replied "of course". And so we were soon past the obstacle and on our way again, rather later than expected.

The 45km to the 'main road', was horrible. In places it had been washed away by the rains so that we had to detour off the road over small makeshift bridges built by other drivers. Soon enough, though, after driving through pineapple plantations, we arrived at the main north road. From here the going is *really* tough!

It was whilst descending the infamous 'hill of fourteen wrecked trucks' that I first noticed the noise. A sort of sharp 'clunk' from the rear. I stopped and crawled around underneath but couldn't see anything out of place. We stopped that night on a football pitch in a small town as camping spots are hard to find in sisal plantations. As I made the sharp turn off the road 'clunk, clunk, clunk ...' "Aaaaargh! What can that be?"

It could only be one thing and that's what I was afraid of ... the differential – my second. I removed the cover and my fears were confirmed. It's lucky we carry a spare, we're the only overland company that does. I finished for the night at 1.30am having worked under the truck solidly since stopping, and was up again at 6am to finish off. At 9am we were on our way.

The road is unrelenting; dips, humps and large holes that are impossible to avoid, keeping our speed down to a crawl and our course erratic. After only 70kms it was lunchtime so I stopped on a flat grassy area by the roadside. I glanced under the truck and noticed that the differential was leaking a bit of oil and then noticed that the right hand end of my front axle was also leaking. I knew what this meant and, on closer inspection, I could see a three inch crack around the axle end. I wasn't annoyed or despairing, even though I knew it would take the rest of the day to replace, just glad that I'd noticed it before it broke. Other drivers have not been so lucky and have had their entire front wheel assembly, hubs, brakes, and all, fall off on the road!

Anyway, pretty soon and not before time, we were out of Tanzania. I don't feel very comfortable there, mainly because of the large amounts of illegal money I have to deal in. The black market exchange is very worthwhile, there being seventeen shillings to one U.S. Dollar in the bank and up to a hundred and sixty-five to a dollar on the street. I entered with fourteen thousand shillings and had soon to buy diesel. The trouble is that most garages do (and all should) ask to see your bank foreign exchange receipts. I chose the seediest-looking place I could, amongst other garages so there'd be some competition. I told the attendant to 'fill it up'. Asking the price per litre I was told it was 10/-. I saw the price on the pump was 9/40 so that was a good sign. The numbers rolled round and round as the proverbial creek got potentially deeper and deeper. I went to the office to ask to use the toilet so I could see whether they had one of those 'ALL FOREIGN VEHICLES MUST SHOW BANK RECEIPTS' notices. I couldn't see one.

Seven hundred litres later, both tanks topped to the brim, I walked boldly, though apprehensively into the office with a wad of 7,000/- shillings plus 3,000/- extra in my pocket in case I needed to bribe my way out of three or four years in prison.

"That's 7000/-, please" he said calmly.

"Here you are, 1, 2, 3, 4, 5, 6 and 7."

"You won't be needing a receipt, will you?"

"Well, I'd just like something to let my boss know where his money has gone."

"The receipt book has been sent away today", he lied. I wasn't about to challenge him. He'd made a pretty good personal profit this morning and I was still a free man so I thanked him and got out of there as quickly as possible.

Then in Dar Es Salaam I had to change more money, so to save everyone from dealing separately with the black marketeers, I collected the money they wanted to change so that I could do it all together; that way you get a better rate anyway. In the past, one walk down the main street would attract at least ten people asking "Change money?" I wouldn't deal with them anyway as they're far too dodgy but it's a good guide to the availability.

Unfortunately, the man I knew at the hotel was away so I had to find a new contact. The best way to go about this is to ask other European travellers where they changed their money and take it from there. I asked some Australians who told me of a travel agent and a hairdresser who would change, but the hairdresser wouldn't do it whilst his wife was at home so we went to the travel agent. After two minutes a friend of mine I'd first met at Victoria Falls and then again on two occasions in Botswana, walked in. He was on his way to Nairobi, hitch-hiking, and was also trying to change money. It seemed as though there had been a big 'clean up the black market' operation. No-one asked me in the street and the man at the travel agency wasn't there anymore.

So it was that Murray and I went to the Greek hairdressers where we asked about changing money. He had a shave that took forty-five minutes, including the wait, until the man's wife went out whereupon we gave him £300. It was all very shady like something out of an old film. My share was 39,000/- which filled a carrier bag. There was a policeman across the road when we left, so we split up in case we were followed and distributed the money as quickly as possible.

This time, in Kenya, I was determined to visit the Marine Park near Malindi. It has become clear to me that Paul, the leader on the previous trips, was actually very reluctant to do anything he didn't have to do or to try anything new. On this trip, however, I have seen as many new places as ones I'd previously visited and have not been pushed for time.

The sea was rough and the wind bent the palm trees like those on films of hurricanes as we pitched our tents at the Adventist Youth camp. The next day the sea was still rough even inside the offshore coral reef when we hired a small glass bottomed boat to view the marine life. The young African didn't seem concerned at the swell as we set off, but I reckoned that he'd have swum the distance for the amount of money he'd be getting!

I wasn't actually too worried as one wave after another crashed over the front of the boat, soaking us all and steadily filling it with water, as it was still a fairly short swim to the shore. The problem was that we were going into the waves. Some of the passengers were having second thoughts, especially as all that could be seen through the glass window in the bottom of the boat was opaque muck.

After about an hour of this we tied up to a buoy and, suddenly, there were hundreds of fish under the boat. Out came the masks and snorkels and soon I was a fish again in the warm, clear Indian Ocean. Beautiful coloured fish looking me straight in the eye, nibbling at my arms, swimming along with me. Weird sea anemones and colourful corals decorated the irregular sea bed. Here all was calm and the anemones slid back and forth gracefully in sympathy with the heavy swell a few feet above. Here it is that I can fly! All too soon we were back in the boat and heading back, now almost surfing the waves.

From Malindi we cut across into Tsavo East National Park where we saw some enormous crocodiles, two cheetahs and terrible roads. Then across into Tsavo West National Park. I decided to camp there at a small rough camp about fifteen minutes' drive into the Park. As we put up our tents and brought the food out on to the table we were watched closely by a large troupe of baboons. The big male, as big as a man, twice as strong and with four hands and fearsome teeth, was getting closer and closer. Next he was in the site amongst the tents, baring his savage teeth to scare everyone into the truck before walking off with a sack of potatoes (which he proceeded to calmly eat sitting against a tree in the camp). That night a loud roaring like that of a lion could be heard close to the camp along with the eerie barking and chanting of the baboons like that heard before at Lake Nakuru.

And so today I have been showing everyone around one of my favourite Parks, Tsavo West, among the volcanoes and lava flows. Today I've found two nature trails that I couldn't find last time I was here. On one of them, going up a volcanic ash cone, I found a tunnel where the lava had flowed out eighty-five years ago. We took torches and explored the interior of the volcano; it was fascinating, the walls and roof dripping petrified molten rock, purple in colour and razor-sharp rocks on the floor.

Nairobi has been very hectic, my old group mostly gone and my new group appeared. I have to get us all the visas for Burundi, Zaire, Central African Republic and Chad. I still hope we won't have to go back through Chad but the visa situation with Nigeria is unpredictable at the moment. I managed to get all it done by 10.00am but I might have guessed that it would take much longer dealing with Zaire. They were on the 12th floor and two lifts stopped working with me in them. I had to push the alarm in one to get out!

So, with two days' wait, I've come back to Lake Nakuru, almost certainly the place you referred to as having seen in 'Out of Africa', with all the flamingos. You'll be pleased to hear that I caught up with your letter to Lusaka. It was whilst sitting on the beach at Cape Maclear in Malawi that I was approached by a man of about sixty. He'd driven his VW Combi Van over from Lusaka and wanted to borrow some Evostik to fix something on it. As I was looking for it, we got chatting. It seemed that he knew Mr. And Mrs. Bland whose farm it is we stay at near Lusaka. I asked if he could deliver a message to them asking if they could pick up the mail. He said that it would probably be easier to pick it up himself as he lived in town, so I gave him a mailing list and some Zambian stamps. I received the letter in Nairobi yesterday. Actually it's been like Christmas, the amount of letters I've received. It's so nice to have resumed contact.

I've read so many letters tonight that I don't think I'll be able to refer back to them so hope I haven't omitted to include anything you asked for. Has my parcel arrived? I expect it to take a long time but I'll be relieved to hear that it has. I have to pick up my trainee driver tomorrow from the airport. Apparently he's an ex-policeman, 'so watch it' my Telex said!

I collected Jim, my trainee, from the airport. I had to wait for an hour-and-a-half, amongst heaving crowds of expectant relatives, clutching an Exodus Brochure for identification. He appeared carrying an Exodus Expeditions hold-all in one hand and a sack of spare parts on his shoulder. We walked back to the truck where Dave, one of my passengers, was waiting in the cab and listening to the cassette player. As I introduced them the music stopped in mid-song.

"Has the tape finished?"
"No, it shouldn't have done"
And then ...
"Can you smell burning?"
The smell of burning plastic quickly filled the air followed by smoke streaming up from behind my seat. I reached back and felt the mass of wires. One was getting very hot. I leapt out. The smoke was getting worse. I could now see the wire glowing red where it had burned away the insulation.

"Pass the pliers". I was afraid it would soon ignite. I tore the wire apart and the panic was over.

"Welcome to the trip, Jim." I joked.
One hundred yards later ...
"I can smell burning again."
"So can I."
I stopped and found another wire was melting and the performance was repeated. That night we disconnected the batteries so cancelling any unplanned midnight barbecues!

Jim seems like a nice enough guy, easy-going and good humoured and, apart from being, for a time, a policeman, he's done a host of other jobs and certainly doesn't wish to be considered the group policeman. I'm sure we're going to get along fine.

Anyway, I'm going to close this letter once and for all so that I can send it tomorrow so all the best to everyone, have a good summer.

Love,
Graham.

Map 7d. East Africa and the Rift Valley.

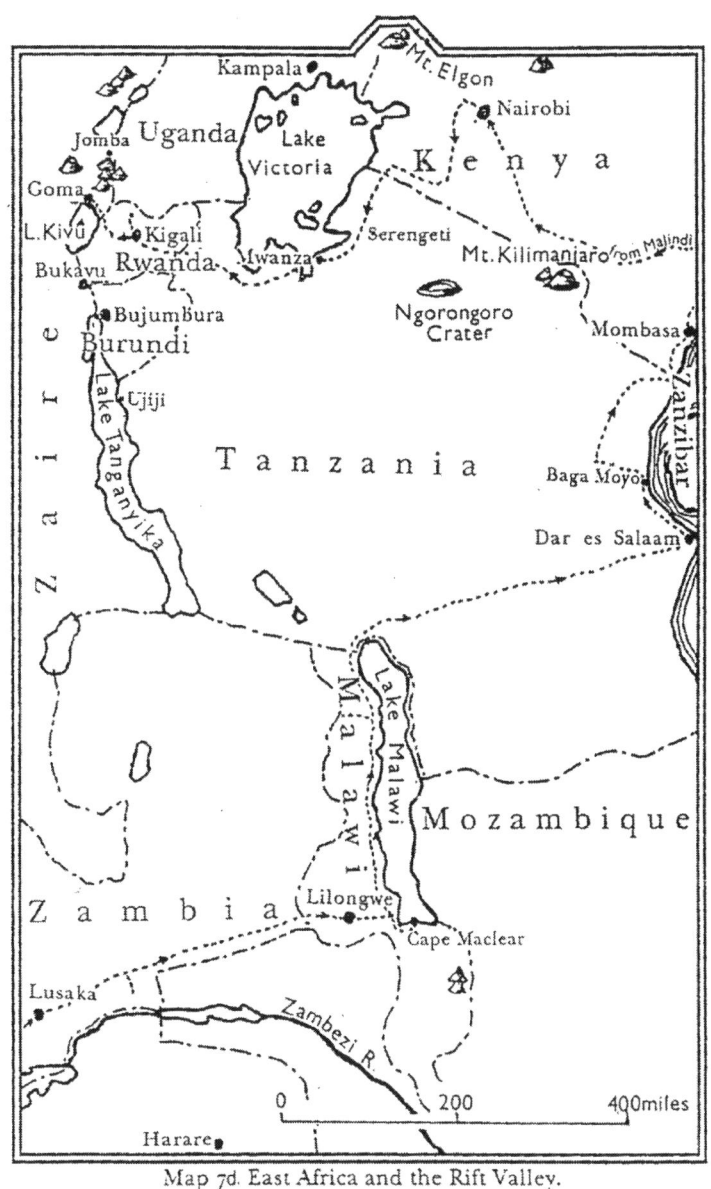

18 July 1986, Near Kigali, Rwanda

Dear All

I seem to have found a bit more time to write now after the hectic craziness of Nairobi. It's taken me all of a week to wind down and I still feel that there's a way to go. What I could really have done with was a week off but unfortunately that's not possible. So I've been trying to take it easy and keep the group together and the trip rolling at the same time. It should have been a great burden removed now that I have Jim, my trainee driver, with me but instead I find that I often have to chase him up for forgetting to do this or that or not putting the tools away properly. It's an interesting phenomenon; I often felt the same way as a trainee - forgetful, absent-minded, even stupid at times. I tried to 'snap out of it' but never could completely – that is, until I was completely in charge. I can't get mad at Jim but would like to figure out why this should be, so that we can do something about it. (I just hope he doesn't lose all the tools first!).

We left Nairobi on the 11th July and drove directly to the Masai Mara game reserve. To make it a bit more interesting I decided to take a back road. One of my passengers, Alex, who is my age and an ex-Army officer (and who can be rather sullen and moody at times) wanted to hitch-hike on to Mwanza in Tanzania. He'd lived in Mwanza years before and would forego the game park for an extra two days there.

At the junction on the dirt track where we were to turn left, I stopped to let him get out. As far as we could see was virtually nothing; two tyre marks in the baked straw coloured plain was the road he intended to travel. Wildebeest, zebra and large herds of cattle were clustered sparsely between here and the horizon. Who knows how many lions were asleep behind the occasional bushes. Actually, I recently heard the story from another driver that they'd seen two lions behind a bush and a little further on seen two Masai women walking their direction. They'd stopped to warn the women by pointing and saying 'Simba, simba'. The women, instead of turning and walking away, suddenly got excited, picked up handfuls of stones and ran to where the lions were, pelting them and shouting until the lions had had enough and slunk away. Bravely, however, Alex struggled into his rucksack, said 'Cheerio' to everyone and walked off into the dusty distance. Would we ever see him again? Time would tell.

That night we camped about 10kms from the park gate so as not to have to pay. As with all the parks, there is no physical boundary and there can easily be as many animals outside it as in. There were many wild noises that evening and after we'd gone to bed a pack of hyenas came into the camp to laugh and chatter and sniff around.

The next day we drove around and saw an abundance of wildlife, ending up for the night at Keekorok Lodge. There was a Guerba Overland truck there so we camped together. Keekorok Lodge is a large collection of huts and buildings; it also houses the Park Headquarters, maintenance people and their families, balloon ride people, etc. It is not fenced off so there is a ban on walking around the lodge – more like a village – after 7pm. We all wanted to go down to the bar for the evening so would have to drive. The Guerba group had already gone to eat there. Shortly after our dinner, at the camp fire, Jim decided to take the spade into the bushes, there being no toilet nearby. Almost immediately he rushed back panicking.

"I've just walked right up to a lion", he said, "I walked round that bush and there it was, right there, three feet from my torch." (It was later speculated that he definitely had not had time to dig a hole!)

Everyone got into the truck and scanned the area with torches but nothing could be seen. As we left for the bar it started to rain heavily. We parked the truck near the gate to the central lodge area, which is as close as we're allowed, and walked to the bar. Soon the rain was bouncing and spraying upwards from the patio outside the French windows of the cosy bar. A large log fire glowed from the stone fireplace as the lightning streaked across the windows and the thunder drowned the conversation. At about 11pm a bedraggled-looking guard came in and asked for the driver of our truck.

"Yes?" I said (What can it be?).

"There are three lions lying next to your truck, two females and one male. I wouldn't go back there just yet".

We were happy to stay for another hour in the bar before eventually, cautiously, returning to find the lions gone.

The following day we drove along the extremely muddy and barely used road to the North West gate, through tens of thousands of wildebeest which have recently migrated from the Serengeti. Soon we were back in Tanzania on our way to Rwanda and Zaire. We weaved and bumped and thudded past the scene of the 'ant adventure' and on to Mwanza. Mwanza is a fairly large, industrial town. Jim was driving and hadn't been here before so I pushed the buzzer for him to stop so that I could jump into the cab and direct him. He duly stopped and I clambered down the side of the truck and into the cab.

"Is that where you arranged to meet him?" asked Jim.

"Who?"

"Alex."

"No, at the Post Office. It's okay, I've got a map."

"Well, we don't need to go there anymore, do we?" Said Jim

"Why not?" I replied

"Because he's already in."

"What do you mean?"

"He just got in."

"Never!"

"I thought that's why you buzzed me", he said.

"No, I buzzed you so that I could get in the cab to direct you".

"Well, you got out one side and, at the same time, he got in at the other!"

Later that day we arrived at the Busisi ferry, which wasn't working when I last came here. Thankfully, it is now, and is also free. After another day's driving we arrived at the Rwandan border.

'Pole, pole (pronounced polie, polie) is a much used Swahili phrase meaning 'Slowly, slowly'. It adequately describes the attitude here and was amply demonstrated on this border, both on the Tanzanian and the Rwandan sides. There were, however, no problems.

So now we are all speaking French and driving the wrong side of the cab. The road to Kigali, the capital, is good but, after only 15km, we were diverted by two policemen down a side road. They assured us that it joined up again further on. 60kms of rough dirt and steep hills later, we asked a truck driver who told us basically that we were now further from Kigali than when we'd started. It didn't really matter though, we just got to see more of Rwanda than we'd intended. As in Malawi, the people are extremely friendly and colourfully dressed. We got to

Kigali on Saturday morning so have to stick around until Monday for Telex, money, etc.

I looked at the map. About 30kms north on the Uganda road is a lake. Visions of a quiet weekend by the lake attracted everyone so we set off to find it. After 80kms we did find it and indeed it was beautiful, if fairly heavily populated around the shore. The rounded hills drop steeply to the long and narrow lake making camping spots hard to find. Eventually we found a grassy spot where I could drive the truck down to the water's edge.

We're the most exciting event that's happened here in living memory! I think that everybody in the valley has visited us now. Our 'quiet' campsite is evidently the local laundry, swimming pool, fishing harbour, cattle watering, pig washing, village water supply and community centre for a large area. (It's been quite good fun, though).

For the first time in weeks, it seems, I've managed to sneak away for a bit of solitude. I actually get to miss my own company sometimes. It's pretty busy in the truck all the time.

"Sorry, can you move so that I can get into my locker?"

"Has anyone seen a light-blue jumper?"

"Scuse me, can I get into my locker?"

"Graham, the cook-light's not working again."

"Can I get into my locker, please?"

"Uuurgh! Who did that? Someone's got rotten guts!"

"Can I get into my locker?"

"Has anyone seen the tin-opener?"

"Scuse me, sorry, scuse me."

"You'll have to move while I get into my locker."

So now I'm sitting in the shade of some woodland overlooking the lake and banana groves with the sound of local

children and my passengers laughing and splashing somewhere in the distance. This is a day I have been looking forward to.
Must go now.
All the best.
Graham.

Map 6b. The Zaire river basin.

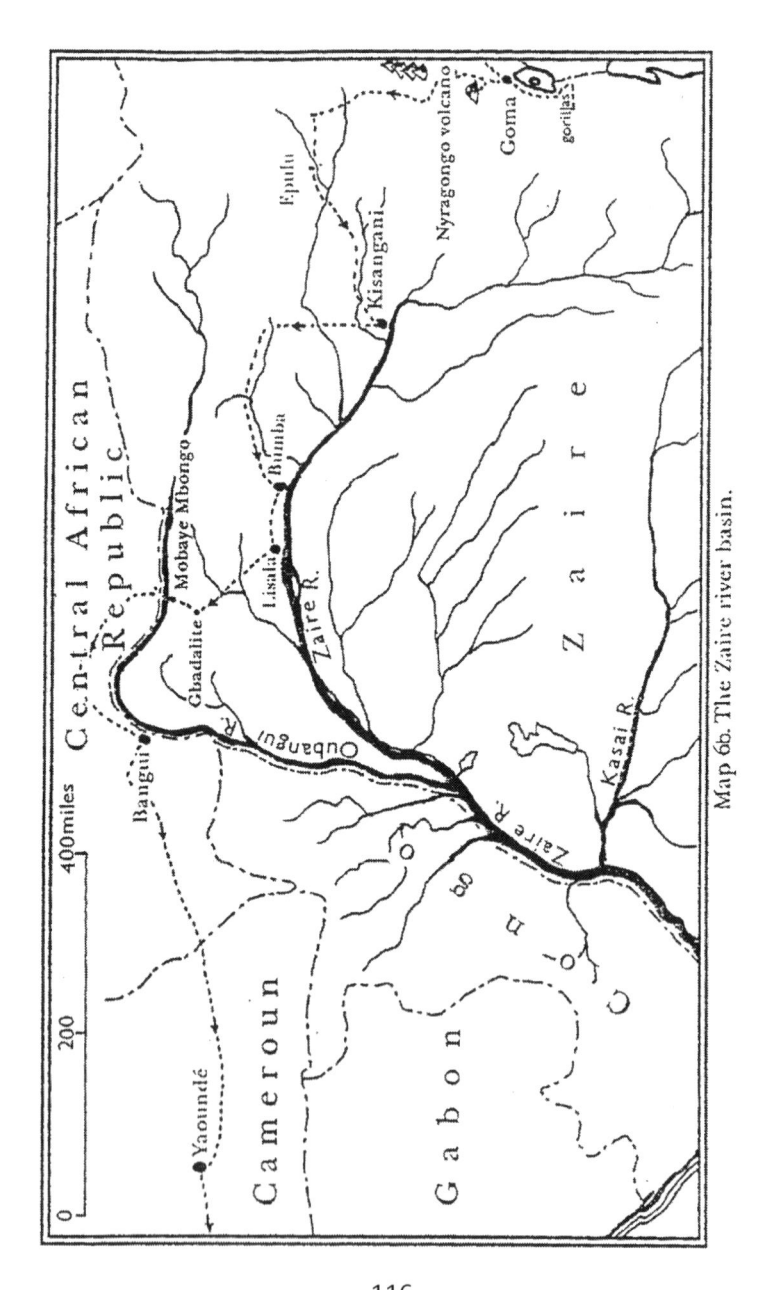

24 July 1986 Bukavu, Zaire

Dear All

All my passengers are presently visiting the gorillas whilst I must stay and guard the truck. It seemed a good opportunity to start a letter even though it's not safe to post it until Bangui.

I got your letter to Goma along with two others – one of which was posted on 4th January! Thanks for the newspaper cuttings. Yet another about South Africa! It's a subject that I know I've written much about but one that I would now like to close. My attitude has changed since visiting South Africa. Previously it was rather simplistic as I believe are attitudes throughout the world, being based solely on heavily opinionated media reports. Black or White? What I see now is that this is not the choice. South African problems are highly complex and deeply rooted in their history. Their history cannot be changed. Their government simply reflects the attitudes of the voting population. Their attitudes can't be changed. They are very much aware, however, of the media attention they are getting and perhaps this is reflected in some of the recent concessions that have been made by the government. Regardless of what they'd really like to see, they are in the unenviable position of having to steer between a black uprising and a white backlash. I don't know if sanctions would do any good or not but I think that the media attention may do by keeping the pressure on and things moving forward.

I don't like the South African system because it fails to recognise what, to me, is plain to see; that all people are born equal and that this equality is not compromised by environmental, social and cultural differences. There is no easy answer. I no longer pretend there is but instead now watch the developments impartially with interest and sometimes with horror.

I thought that it may be interesting if I included in this letter some of the things I've written over the past few months. They're not in any particular order :-

The first was written during the breakdown at Victoria Falls. 22nd April 1986:

I strolled easily down the now familiar footpath along the ridge opposite the Eastern Cataract. There were a great many more people than usual, dressed up for the day out – smiles, smart colours, suits and ties. I, however, now accustomed to the conditions here, was securely wrapped in my hooded raincoat, shorts and sandals. With the change of wind it was, surprisingly, much drier today, even though the river was approaching full flood, making it, for once, possible to walk right to the edge, hardly getting wet at all.

I was thinking as I walked, contemplating my conversation around the camp fire the previous night. Wondering about travelling without a camera in order to more clearly describe the scenes I see by using words.

"The problem," I considered, "is that of inspiration".

But perhaps I deny myself inspiration by using such an instant art form as photography. I thought to attempt to describe the scenes that I would otherwise have photographed. Today would be a good day as I had deliberately come without my camera for safety from possible robbery...

The scene was revealed to me through a tunnel of undergrowth, drawing me to its end. As usual, it looked different today, appearing through a window in the heavy swirling spray, framed, fading to white as in a movie dream scene or Victorian family portrait...

Hung above, instead of bright, clear sky, were pregnant, dirty purple bellies of cloud, in dark, matt contrast to the billowing all around.

Viewed, as it was, on a level with the unsuspecting upper river, a line of miniature palm trees and scrub, otherwise in perfect perspective with their placid surroundings, edged that monstrous precipice, belying its tremendous scale. And from here the solid brown masses of river rush recklessly down and over in slow motion, turning to white vapour waves and sheets freefalling in weightless suspension down – down – down until they explode to drenching dust on the rocky protrusions far below.

Perhaps because I'm mainly water myself, I feel the powerful urge to join in and jump, shouting unheard into the pounding, deafening roar. To fall in careless submission to the overwhelming wrath of this movie-dream scene, to make the dream real and complete; as if it were not already so...

The next was written during my first visit to Zaire on 15 January 1986:-

I saw a little black boy with such enthusiastic, lively, loving eyes and clear and joyful smile that I couldn't tear my gaze away, for he seemed so unbelievably familiar. But here I was, eight-thousand miles away from home and he didn't look like anyone I knew. Yet it struck me that I know him better than I know myself.

This one was written in Muyinga, Burundi about a beautiful woman who was by the truck:

Proud negress,	Uncommon Language
Slender temptress,	And uncommon land
Ragged princess,	But for a moment
Blooming maturity,	I find the tower of Babel stands
New-found surety,	You'll stay with me for ever
Nervously confident.	Though we'll never meet again

The next one speaks for itself:

Whilst camping by a mud road in Africa,
I heard a crackling news report from England
Which said that the 25th Space Shuttle mission
Had ended in disaster in the USA.
"America is shocked and stunned"
Seven innocent people died for the betterment of mankind.
But how many others died silently at the same time
Because of mankind's inequality and greed?

I wrote this at the "Carnivore" restaurant and disco in Nairobi:-

The thin, grey-haired white man danced awkward and self-consciously with his well-dressed and attractive negress pick-up. Doubtless, herself a good and vigorous dancer socially, tonight looked around and very bored. He had already paid lavishly from his racial privilege for the gluttonous dinner they had picked at with mutual insincerity; patterns that would inevitably continue later into the night.

I wrote the next one about the couple whose place we stay at in the Okavango Delta:

They lived deep in the swamps of Botswana,
With a bar and a swimming pool.
They had a very young child that they both loved, sometimes rather embarrassingly with "Goo, goo" baby talk.
Insofar as blending of cultures is concerned it must be said that she did breastfeed.
Even in public.
And she did occasionally carry the child on her back, albeit in an extravagant chair.
But, for the most part, the innocent white baby plumply peered through the wooden bars of its cage.
Of course, it had everything that it might possibly want
Knee-deep in every plastic and squeaky, furry thing money could buy and watched contemptuously by the hired African baby-minder, herself reared, often naked, carried on her sister's back, with work to do and tin cans for toys.
Wearily she would poke another plaything through the bars.
Though she did try once, unsuccessfully, to get the child to dance.

*   *   *

Well, we got through Zaire safely, leaving yesterday 11th August. After leaving the gorillas I had to buy two new tyres for the truck as we'd burst one of the nearside ones on the road from Goma. At £250 a piece it's made a big dent in my funds.

So again we drive the 180kms alongside Lake Kivu to Goma, twisting amongst the steep green hills of this fantasy landscape, dodging holes and rocks, overlooking banana grove islands in the glassy lake. As for swimming, it's one of the most pleasant lakes in Africa, warm, clear and clean (though infested with bilharzia). Next stop is the volcano.

We'd heard stories that it's actually erupting but it turned out that it's the one adjoining Nyiragongo that is active. It's still possible to climb that one but the porters want a fortune for taking the risk. Jim and I had to stay down and look after the truck whilst everyone else wheezed and slogged their way up Nyiragongo, returning the next morning. The whole area was muffled in a heavy haze and an indistinct dark mass issued ominously from the adjacent cone. That night we found an excellent camping spot by Rutshuru Falls where we were once again able to jump in, cool down and wash clothes.

We've found the Zaire roads, the main ones anyway, to be in remarkably good shape this time. The rickety bridges have been fixed and the holes filled in. In one day we covered what had taken two-and-a-half days the last time I was here. Soon we were in Epulu to see the pygmies. This time I was able to arrange that we walk for ten miles into the jungle and stay the night at a remote pygmy encampment.

So, led by a barefoot pygmy with a bow and arrow and tailed by a soldier with a gun, we filed in crocodile through the rain forest. Many of the group had found it hard to heed my advice as to what not to take and were kitted out with smart walking boots, clean, dry socks and heavy packs. After only 10 minutes we were knee-deep in streams and swamps and mud; they soon gave up trying to hop from dry patch to the next and sploshed carefree along the route of my sandals! I was moved to write about one of my group:

Max, the twentieth-century giant, had his birthday with the pygmies.
A four-hour hike through the jungle of Zaire.
A night spent in awesome stone-age woods,
A night akin to Lilliput or Hobbiton.
But all he saw was mud.
People reassured him,
"Wow! It's one you'll not forget"
It's true, and he'll be telling all his friends of when his boots got wet; show a tedium of photographs of how he got them all to pose.
But to Chartered Accountancy, the culture and the history

The basis of our ancestry, is lost amongst
The forest trees and mud and rain and film
And brand new boots and too much luggage.
And anyway, isn't really interested and doesn't want to know.

    After four hours of barely distinguishable trails and having passed through two abandoned pygmy camps we emerged into a small clearing. At least, the area was clear on the ground although the high canopy was virtually unbroken. Arranged in a rough circle were maybe eight dwellings; domes of brown leaves, open at one side with a smouldering fire in each opening. Four or five women with babies were busy cooking or gossiping. They bade us welcome and we all sat on our bags wondering what was going to happen next. One by one, the men returned and shook everyone's hand. In appearance they are quite unlike the other Africans of the area. Apart from being obviously much shorter, they are generally rather hairy and often have a large paunch of a belly even though they may otherwise be skinny. Soon the camp was full of people and, although there were eleven of us, they seemed to carry on pretty much as normal, arguing, shouting at the children, kicking the dogs, joking, laughing and chatting. Each of them, it appeared, had a pile of offal or piece of an animal wrapped up in banana leaves which they cooked for themselves. There didn't seem to be a definite meal. We'd taken a bucketful of vegi-stew and they were as happy to eat that as anything else without the least sign of surprise or the vaguest comment. The soldier and a pygmy returned from a short hunting expedition with a large monkey which was put onto one of about fifteen fires to burn off the fur and to cook. It looked more and more human as the fur burned away and the thought of eating it didn't appeal to anyone except the pygmies.

The night drew in and all the little fires glowed in the laughing faces around them. One boy produced a musical instrument, like a bow that he played with a stick whilst blowing on the string. Very Aboriginal, noted the Australians. Many of the pygmies were smoking marijuana in large pipes of which even the women partook. We sat talking and taking in this magic scene, a tiny speck of light in this immense rain forest. Suddenly the chief shouted out something and it was bedtime. Some of the group had been offered places in huts whilst the rest of us lay around the fire on the clear, warm night and soon we were all asleep.

I was woken in the morning by the sound of the Chief, outside whose hut I'd slept, performing a loud soliloquy in between puffing on his pipe, coughing and spitting. Everyone was lying still if not asleep and nobody appeared to be listening to him.

Once up and ready, the pygmy men and boys slung their coiled nets onto their heads and we left with them for a morning's work. They had soon arranged the nets in a line end-to-end between the trees and undergrowth and chased a fairly large gazelle into them. We arrived at that moment whereupon they asked somebody for a knife. Wolfgang, our avid, meat-eating German quickly produced his Swiss Army knife and watched distastefully as it was used to saw deep to the spine, into the throat of the unfortunate creature. After this, it was bundled into a basket and carried by our pygmy guide back to Epulu where it would be exchanged for other foodstuffs.

An excellent book on the subject of the Epulu pygmies is *The Forest People* by Colin Turnbull published by Jonathan Cape.

Onwards to Kisangani...

The roads not quite so good now. At one point Jim hit a big bump and Dave, who was sitting at the back, bashed his head on one of the steel bars supporting the overhead luggage racks. We had to pull three local trucks out of mud holes in order to continue. The next day, without warning, Dave was sick in the truck – he looked terrible – and I knew immediately that he had concussion and that it could be very serious. I was glad to have a student surgeon amongst my passengers who examined him. He said that as it was delayed concussion it was probably not too serious but that we ought to try and get him to a doctor, if possible. We pulled into the Olympia Hotel at Kisangani and took Eugene, a local lad who runs errands for us, to show us to a doctor (ha, ha!). The first place we went only had an 'assistant doctor' as the other had gone off for the day. All he wanted to do was treat Dave for malaria so we tried to find a certain Spanish doctor who was having siesta and his guard wouldn't wake him. We decided to see how Dave looked next morning and he went to bed immediately we got back to the hotel.

The facilities for camping at the hotel are, to say the least, grotty. The shower is like a cave with black mould and cockroaches on the walls and just a trickle of water from the stark, roseless, protruding pipe. In Britain you choose the toilet with the seat, the paper and the lock on the door. Here you choose the one that is least close to overflowing, is in more or less one piece and needs the minimum of paddling to reach it!

Nevertheless, this place is an oasis in the jungle where you can relax over a beer for a few days and swap stories with other travellers. It seemed that out timing was spot on; there were several other travellers with Land Rovers and motorcycles who had been waiting over two weeks for the infamous Zaire River steamer. By comparing all the differing information we had received we reckoned it would be leaving on the Tuesday – in two days' time. I spent all of Monday morning in the bank trying to change money after which I went to the steamer ticket office to buy tickets for my passengers.

There was a large crowd of people standing around the welded steel grille which formed one wall of the empty room behind. There were some French people from the hotel waiting and they said that there was only one man who could sell tickets and he wasn't there.

At length he returned and those who recognised him were pushing and shoving even before he'd entered the office. I was in the second row and determined to hold my position. The people in the front row all had both arms through the grille clutching money and bits of paper. The second row had maybe one arm through and the third row perhaps a hand or else were holding the grille and pulling themselves forward. The French girl in front of me was getting served at last and the man at the desk was calmly writing down all her passport details into the elaborate ticket machine.

"Hmm," I thought, "I don't have anyone's passport. Never mind, I'm not giving up now."

I figured that, when she extricated herself, I could squeeze into her space. What I hadn't reckoned on was that three other people had the same idea. The jostling started as soon as she got served; not just the English 'stick-a-shoulder-in-and-hope-no-one-notices' trick, but not far short of a fight, pushing and writhing into no gaps at all. I lost, and the crowd was so tightly packed that I couldn't move in any direction in the thick, sweaty heat and could honestly have picked up my feet without falling down. (For future reference I did see one guy hold out three cigarettes with his money and get served straight away!). I gave up, not wanting to eventually get served only to be asked for the passports I didn't have, and walked back to the hotel. I told the group to go with their passports and try to get their own tickets as I was trying to sort out another problem...

The truck had been belching black smoke for a long time and had been using more and more engine oil of late. Also an unhealthy ticking noise had developed. The previous day we had removed the cylinder head and found, just like the ill-fated truck at Victoria Falls, a hole in a piston. The only thing to do was to run on five cylinders but this time I wouldn't remove the damaged one, just clean it and take off the broken rings, take the tappets and push-rods out and feed the diesel from the injector pump back to the tank. It worked well but was, for us, another excuse to put the truck on the steamer even though it would cost us out of our wages. I went back to the ticket office to try and glean some information. Everyone I saw sent me to someone else until, at last, I thought I'd found the Chief. In French he told me that there wasn't enough room for the truck on the boat so, pleased at least to have a definite answer, prepared myself mentally for the five-hundred mile drive around on some of the worst roads in Zaire on five cylinders.

After four hours most of the group had got their tickets and had then to go through immigration formalities. I was never quite sure why as no-one is leaving Zaire yet and we don't need to do it if we drive.

Back at the hotel, Dave seems to have perked up and says he feels up to the boat ride. Some people with a Land Rover then asked me if the chief had spoken English. I told them that he hadn't. They said that the chief they'd seen was the only helpful person there, spoke good English and said that they could put thirty vehicles on the boat. They were quite certain that, if I spoke to him, there'd be no problem with the truck. So next morning, Tuesday, I drove everyone down to the docks and went to find the chief. He's an elusive man but I eventually tracked him down and he said there'd be no problem. However, no sooner had he said this than the other chief I had spoken to previously came in and told him that there wasn't enough room.

"Come back this afternoon," he said, "when they've finished loading everything else. Then we'll see if there's room."

"When do you expect the boat to leave?" I asked.

"Maybe tomorrow. I don't know."

We went back in the afternoon to find that they'd hardly started unloading the barge, let alone loaded it. Next morning, early, we returned and I'd got everyone to pack their rucksacks as though the truck wasn't going. We'd heard that when the Captain is ready, the boat simply leaves, ready or not – so we weren't taking any chances. The motorcyclist and Land Rover people had slept on the quayside and, of course, were still there – as was the steamer.

The steamer is huge. It consists of several barges, some with cabins and gallery walkways, some flat cargo barges arranged in a group rather than a line and pushed through the water by the powerful rear section with towering bridge and somewhat misnamed first-class cabins. It has a floating population of people whose livelihood it is to trade on the boat with the passengers and there are also the pirogues or dug-out canoes that come from every village on the river to catch up with the steamer to trade. Everywhere people were washing clothes, selling vegetables or just sitting around but this was before the passengers had embarked.

I found the chief and he came down to the barge to have a look and then said that the truck could go on. Now it was all go...

I sent Jim to change more money. I pushed and shoved in the ticket queue to buy my ticket. I cleared immigration.

Everyone unpacked their gear again. I went into the relevant office and filled in a long form and paid my money (a lot). I then went down to the goods shed and filled in another long form. I persuaded the policeman on the gate to let the truck into the loading area. Then... we waited... and waited...

The barge was still being unloaded. We lazed around, had lunch and heard from several people that the boat wasn't likely to leave until the next day. Some of my group wandered off up to the ice-cream shop they'd found in town, some others went to a bar.

MOOOOOOOOOOOOOOOOOOOOOO! The steamer boomed.

We all wondered why they should be sounding the ship's horn. The quayside was now a mass of people running this way and that, panicking.

"Ha ha" we thought. "They all think it's about to leave. Little do they know they've got to load this barge yet."

MOOOOOOOOOOOOOOOOOOOOOO!...............MO OOOOOOOOOOOOOOO!

I strolled down to where the gangplank was perched precariously. Seven feet long, two feet wide with no hand-rails or anything and thirty feet over the deadly dark gorge between metal and concrete. It was the only way onto the boat and, at either end, was a jabbering, shouting, pushing and panicking crowd of people from which a constant stream was crossing in both directions and clutching each other for stability.

I watched, disbelievingly, for five minutes before turning away, not wanting to see someone fall. I'm quite sure that several people must have fallen.

Every flat space was three deep with people waving to the ten deep crowd on the quayside. I wandered back to the truck and saw that the chief was standing looking at the half-empty barge. I went across and asked him when we would be loaded. The only way to get loaded is by crane and I was looking forward only to the photographs and not the event. He told me that this barge would not now be going with the steamer as it wasn't ready and the steamer was leaving NOW!

"Grab your gear and get on that boat 'cos it's just about to leave." I flapped to the group. "Where's Caroline and Barrie?"

"They're at the ice-cream shop."

"And Chris and John?"

"I think they're at a bar."

MOOOOOOOOOOOOOOOOOOOOOOOOO!

"And Benny's gone for a walk."

Various people sprinted around the town to round everyone up whilst the steamer untied and manoeuvred the barges to be tied on. One of the third Class barges was drifting solo by now, so, in order to position it next to the main barge, the Captain rammed it in the bows at $90°$ to bring it into line. As he did this the whole conglomeration shuddered and I saw at least one of the many thousands of people there, fall overboard. They were between two barges which were rapidly coming together like a hammer to an anvil. People on the boats were all leaning out holding out their hands and shouting, or just looking. I don't know if they got out in time; I couldn't look.

Next to be attached was the flat cargo barge that, after much argument, had now got a Land Rover and a motorbike on board. The steamer manoeuvred itself alongside and, before they even met, hundreds of people had leaped across the gap and started spreading out tarpaulins or sheets for their stalls. I heard later that these are the ruffians of the boat, the wheelers, dealers. A woman snatched up another's sheet and threw it overboard, then placed down her own; there then started a fight involving every member of two families, pulling hair and throwing each other's things overboard. Now everyone on one side of the steamer and everyone on the quayside was watching and cheering or laughing. It is very unusual for Africans to behave so badly in public and it was obviously quite a spectacle. My passengers, who had by now all arrived, gasping and ill-equipped, were able to hop across these barges and get aboard just in time as it then turned itself around and churned off downstream towards Lisala.

For me the panic was off and I had now to calmly wade knee-deep into chaotic bureaucracy to try and retrieve my money. The chief said that the barge that they were to put the truck on would, instead, be leaving tomorrow by cargo boat. He pointed it out, it having just arrived.

"It leaves at 2pm," he said.

"Definitely?" I asked stupidly.

"Definitely!" came the reply.

Okay, so we decided to go on the boat after all, having paid our money, to save ourselves the hassle of driving around and trying to get the money back. He told us to be back at 8am to be loaded.

At 8am we arrived back at the docks. The chief wasn't in his office so I went on to the quayside to see who I could find. It was all very quiet this morning.

Quiet, that was, except for a small group of women sitting on the quayside crying. I walked past them and looked over the edge. On the deck of a moored barge, beneath one of the grey steel cranes, a man lay dead. Apparently he had fallen from the crane. The work of unloading containers was going on around him. The police on the gate were, as usual, checking passes and vehicle entry documents. The women wailed and small groups of people would just come to look at the body out of curiosity, then drift away again.

I went to see the captain of the cargo boat and he told me they were definitely not leaving today, or tomorrow or even the day after that. Amazingly enough, when I found the chief, he helped me get my money back within twenty minutes. We bought diesel from the Catholic Mission and left this crazy town, but not before being fined 500 zaires (£5.50) for a completely harmless moment of confusion on a roundabout. Of course, you don't get receipts for fines paid unless you want to spend all day at the Police Station!

The road started fair to poor, we had lunch on the move and didn't stop until 10.00pm. The next morning we met Stewart, who was the main reason for the breakdown of the truck at Victoria Falls. He was flown home from Zambia to be palmed off onto Tracks Overland Co. – a notorious budget operation. He was seven weeks late. He'd had to rebuild his engine in Spain where he'd found half a paintbrush inside it! None of his passengers had any visas so he'd had to go through Chad. When he tried to leave Chad to go into Cameroun they wouldn't let him in without visas – they had recently stopped selling them on the border. So the passengers were stranded for two weeks in no-man's land whilst Stewart managed to talk his way back into Chad and fly to Bangui to get visas. These were just *some* of the problems! The passengers also didn't like Stewart or each other and he'd now almost run out of diesel and money!

The road, in places, was dreadful. One deep mud-hole after another, four-wheel drive for long stretches, deep pools, gullies and washed-away sections. It made for interesting driving. It poured with rain too, making the irregular surface slippery and, eventually, at dusk, we slid off the edge of the narrow track into a soft ditch. It took about two hours to get out and then, ten minutes later, we came across another truck which had done the same except that this one was right down on its chassis. We managed to squeeze round him without slipping off the other side and continued again until 10pm. On the third day we found another heavily loaded truck stuck, blocking our way, in a mud-hole. We pulled him out backwards and then overtook him and pulled him right through whilst he tried to bump-start it. Sometimes these Bedfords are like tanks (mind you, the clutch smelled a bit hot for a while!). Five hundred miles and three days after leaving Kisangani we arrived in Lisala. The boat had arrived in the morning and we arrived at about 9.30pm.

We picked up our group, who told us many stories of continuing craziness on the boat. We camped that night and left early in the morning. The road north to the border at Mbeye-Mbongo is not too bad. We'd have normally gone the much shorter route through Zongo but Stewart had already gone to considerable trouble and inconvenience to find out that a ferry is not working, thus forcing a long, tedious detour. Our road north, however, passes through the President's home village of Gbadalite and for 200kms each collection of huts has a name plaque and the number of kilometres to this most special place. Bumpy dirt track, flanked by continuous rain forest, was interspersed by red mud huts, thatched, with waving children and women cooking on open fires. Suddenly, at the end of the count-down – WHOOSH – and we're unexpectedly on an immaculate dual-carriageway, street lights, avenues of trees, modern office buildings, large airport, very well stocked, though expensive, French supermarket, flash cars, traffic lights and illuminated signposts. It's just like being in a small affluent French town, then , at the other end of the town – ZAPP – and we're back in the jungle with the mud huts and wondering if we really saw all that or did we fall asleep.

The Zaire exit formalities were easy and the ferry across the Oubangui river fairly efficient, if a rip-off. The Central African immigration officer turned up after almost an hour and I went with him into the ten-foot by six-foot tin shed which is the Immigration Office. The inescapable humidity of the afternoon had now darkened the sky to a looming shadow of solid storminess. As this burst open, the roads filled with water like nothing I've ever seen before, the shed filled with people sheltering. There was no light or windows, only gloom coming in through the door, so the immigration officer could hardly see what he was doing with our passports and any form of talking or asking for information by anyone was futile as the lashing, gusting downpour, which had, by now, reduced visibility outside to a few feet of whiteness, made a deafening white noise on the corrugated roof. The thunder and lightning came together in flashing gunfire (always glad to hear it as they say you don't hear the one that hits you!). I leaned forward and glanced out to the truck where I saw all my passengers, dressed only in underwear, leaping around and lying in the torrents rushing down the road!

We waited most of the afternoon for the police to stamp our passports and then got stopped at one of the many 'rain barriers' for the night. The people with the Land Rover were also here. It turns out that they've been living in Zimbabwe but actually come from Watchet! They'd had their Land Rover bashed unloading it off the boat. It also had two deep grooves on the bonnet made by the steel hawser. They said I should be glad I hadn't put the truck on the boat as the equipment at Lisala wasn't very big or strong and they had serious doubts as to whether it could handle even their Land Rover. The Central African rain barriers are proving to be a real hassle and they often only want bribes anyway. At 7am one morning we were told that we'd have to stay at one until 12.00. Twenty cigarettes brought him down to 11am, forty to 10am, sixty to 9am and eighty to 8am. The road is perfectly good, though I can appreciate that it's a good idea.

We arrived in Bangui on a public holiday so I couldn't apply for our Cameroun visas until the next day, Thursday. Now I find that Friday is also a public holiday and there's a rumour that Monday is too. This now puts me about a week behind, though works out quite neatly as people joining in Douala cannot get flights until 26th August and they can also bring my spare parts.

Anyway, this letter has gone on a long time, there's now our daily thunderstorm in progress and the generator is failing so that the lights keep going out in the bar where I'm sitting. The candle I was given has burned away and dinner must be nearly ready by now so...

All the best to everyone,

Love
Graham.

Near Douala, Cameroun.
24th August, 1986.

Dear All,

Once again this is one of my few days off. We're waiting for our Nigerian visas this time and so have come to a place called Limbe on the West African coast where huge, warm Atlantic breakers crash onto the black volcanic sand.

To start on a negative note, I'd like to tell you about some of the corruption, especially in the French speaking half of Africa. I'm not sure it's entirely fair to categorise it like that but it does seem that way, with the possible exceptions of Rwanda and Nigeria.

The policeman in Zaire about whom I wrote in my last letter was the first obvious example; the next was at Bangui, apart from the rain barrier officials. One of my group was leaving from Bangui airport as it was the only flight available for her. One evening at around 9pm I drove out to the airport with a couple of my passengers to find out the plane departure times. The car park was deserted. There were two armed and uniformed guards standing in the main doorway so we drove around and stopped right outside, jumped out and left the engine running. We asked them when the next flight to Paris was leaving. They gave a short unhelpful reply and then asked to see the vehicle documents. I sighed and went rooting around in my locker to find them whilst they got impatient and told me to hurry up. They then wanted to see our passports so I produced them as well. Next they were writing down details and talking about the 'infraction' (offence). I asked them what we'd done wrong and they said that we'd parked in the wrong place and would have to pay 15,000 CFA (about £30)! We couldn't believe it and argued strongly; the price started to come down a little. We continued arguing for forty minutes and got away without paying after we convinced them that we hadn't had time to change any money, having only entered the Central African Republic that day.

The following day a German couple travelling in a Land Cruiser hit a taxi in town and damaged two of its doors. They're quite sure the taxi driver deliberately contrived the 'accident' but, as foreigners, must expect to take the blame. The Germans wanted to play it all straight. Like us they hadn't yet had the chance to buy insurance (which anyway isn't compulsory) but wanted to see everyone right. They were dogged, however, by everyone involved - the police, the taxi-driver and the garage owner who would repair the taxi - all trying to extort as much money as possible from them. They had a week of hassles which involved paying off the police and arguing with the garage owner, who wanted an unreasonable amount of money before taking the advice of all the other travellers on the campsite and clearing off. Two other Germans we met at the campsite had started a business driving trucks to Cameroun and Central Africa and selling them. They'd just finished their fourth run after many months when their truck was stolen. They reported the theft to the police who, to their disbelief, produced documents to prove that the truck wasn't theirs. They'd lost everything they'd made and weren't sure what to do next.

Another friend we've met again and again is Helmut who is travelling on a motorbike. One day in Bangui he'd had the locked box on his bike broken into and all his spares stolen. What annoyed him most, though, was that the town was busy and several people must have watched the theft. No-one would admit to having seen anything. In this respect Bangui is different from most African towns where to shout "Thief" at anyone would be to condemn them to a lynching or stoning, such is the contempt that most Africans have for thieves.

We were all glad to leave Bangui and that night camped near the impressive Boali waterfalls. When I was last here the water was low and the influx of French tourists high; this time was different. We were camped 3kms downstream amid the undergrowth, the roar of the waterfall and the full moon. After dinner we decided, three of us, to walk to the Falls in the bright, blue night. The path was tricky and the dogs outside the huts jumpy; the roar got louder. Ghostly cartoon fairytale waterfall, like a Roger Dean painting, unreal in deep blue monochrome moonlight. A hundred cascades pouring hither and thither from the top of this towering broken rock and issuing from tunnels halfway down. Dark silhouetted trees cling precariously to the many vertical islands in this full torrent of water.

A day and a half later we arrived at Berberati, the last town before the border. We stopped at the market to buy food and then left, hoping to camp just short of the border 100kms away. The road was badly pot-holed and soon we were stopped at an army check point which we are now accustomed to. No sooner had we stopped than a policeman in a pickup truck pulled up alongside and started shouting at us. A little bewildered, we asked him to slow down so that we could understand what he was saying. He claimed we'd almost forced him off the road whilst he was overtaking and that he had blared his horn at us and that, anyway, he was a policeman and had demanded to be allowed to pass. We were quite sure that he hadn't tried to overtake, or sounded his horn, before we'd stopped – and the people in the back of my truck confirmed this. He took Jim's driving licence and told us to follow him to the office. About 2kms along the road he flagged us down and introduced us to the chief, a fat man dressed in fatigues with a maroon beret, who listened to the officer's accusations whilst rocking on his chair. At length he told us we'd have to pay 12,000CFA for the infarction. I asked if we would get a receipt and he said that the police station was closed until 7.30am so we'd have to spend the night there. It was only 1pm and we couldn't spare the time so I asked why it wasn't possible to pay now and go. He said that it was possible. How much? – 6,000 CFA. I grudgingly paid and left, feeling annoyed.

It took three hours and three police stations to leave Central Africa and only one hour and one policeman to enter Cameroun though, if we thought this was the shape of things to come, we were to be proved wrong.

As I noted the last time I was here, the people are exceptionally friendly, in stark contrast to the officialdom. Soon we came across the first police check; vehicle documents, passports, etc., followed closely by the first army check. Same again, with sometimes a light search. On the first day in Cameroun we were stopped maybe eight times by various officials. Next day, approaching Yaounde, on about our fifth check that day, a Gendarme noticed the animal horns we'd bolted to the front of the truck.

"Where's your permit for this game trophy?" he demanded.

"Well, we don't have one. We bought them from somebody in Central Africa."

It had actually been as we were waiting at a Central African rain barrier that we'd swapped them for a packet of cigarettes. They were from a goat or some similar animal and were very old. He ordered us to take them down so that he could see, which was quite an ordeal as they were securely bolted with two inaccessible bolts inside the cab roof. We did as he said. Another officer asked who was the chief and, when I owned up, he took my passport over to their hut. I followed. He was busy writing down my particulars on a form. I looked over his shoulder and noticed I was named as 'the delinquent'! He was filling in the section headed 'nature of infraction'.

"What infraction?" I asked.

"These." He pointed at the horns that were now on the table.

"We bought them in Central African Republic from somebody, not in Cameroun."

"We don't know that" he said stubbornly. "You have no licence for hunting or for this game trophy. Where are your guns?"

"We don't have guns and it's not a trophy. It's just a decoration for the truck and you can keep it. It's not that important."

One of them had got a list of offences and was looking for the amount we'd have to pay.

"Seventy thousand CFAs" he said calmly (about £140).

"That's crazy."

Another one of the policemen was laughing at the hopeless situation they'd put us into and another indicated that, if we gave some 'smaller money' then perhaps the whole thing could be forgotten. Of course! All they wanted were bribes. I was in no mood for giving any more bribes.

"When would the court case be?" I asked.

"The date will be sent to you. You must report to the police station in Yaounde."

I asked if they'd finished with my passport and slowly snatched it back. I noticed that they'd written my name as 'Mr Paul Graham'. They never asked for an address.

And so we left, with all our documents, though not our goat horns, having paid nothing, but still not quite sure if we'd won the day. Though in the absence of police cars, mopeds or radios we reckoned we'd be okay.

The road from Yaounde to Douala is fairly new, smooth tarmac just like any new 'A' road at home. The difference is that it is littered with wrecked vehicles. Not just bumped and banged, but horrifyingly mangled lumps of metal. One appalling smash-up after another, vehicles' remains lying where they'd come to rest, making each terrible sequence of events plain to see. I suppose British roads would look much the same if wrecks weren't removed the same day. I'd like to say that these sights make people drive more safely but no – they're still crazy!

It wasn't until I contacted Exodus from Douala that I heard of the mysterious gas disaster near Wüm in Cameroun. We listened to the radio that night and heard that an estimated two-thousand people had died. Looking at the map, it seemed we were to have gone almost up to the lake and may even have visited it. It's a good job that we're running a week late. Now I think my route will have to change but there's a complete lack of local information. People know that something has happened but no-one really knows what, as there are virtually no newspapers or radios here.

One thing I miss with this job is the weekend. There's never any relaxation, even on days like today, as I always have to be 'Mr Exodus Expeditions' and am always responsible for everything. I wonder how much you'll think I've changed when I return. I feel I've changed a lot and I hope all for the better. I think I'm going to find it hard to get back into some sort of 'normal' life in Britain. Letters I've had from passengers on only the six-week trips say they've found it very strange to be home again.

Latest on the disaster: it's not where we originally thought. The lake isn't even on our map and is more remote. We shouldn't, therefore, have to change our route or go anywhere near the area.

Anyway, all the best to all,
Graham.

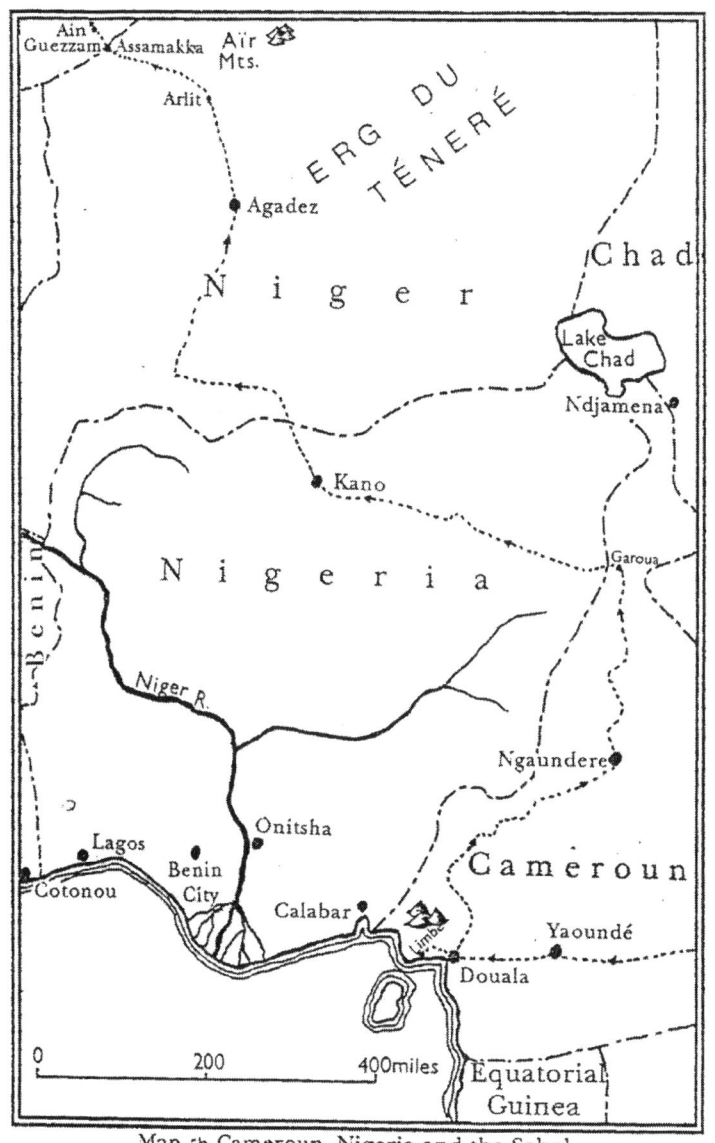

Map 5b. Cameroun, Nigeria and the Sahel.

Kano, Nigeria. 11th September 1986

Dear All,

You will no doubt be relieved to hear that I escaped from Cameroun with my liberty and am, gladly, not one of the thousands of unfortunates reportedly languishing in jail there without trial.

We left Douala with only six passengers; the guy who was to have joined us (and bring my engine parts) has had some back trouble and so couldn't come. This meant, of course, that I still had a sick engine. Bedfords are uncommon in Cameroun so I had to drive to Kano, Nigeria on five cylinders. It runs okay but lacks power and is using twice as much fuel as it should do.

I felt pretty low as we left. It had been raining almost constantly in the drab town and we'd now left three of our liveliest people behind as their trip had finished. We passed about 100kms from Wüm where the widely reported disaster had struck and we met several people who had suffered bereavement. We were twice mistaken for aid workers as there have been so many.

The scenery steadily became more cheering; conical hills and volcanoes, wild areas, brightly coloured craftwork on display outside houses, inexplicable complex corrugated iron spires on even the most ordinary dwellings. The topographical flavour is fast changing from the flat central rain forests. Fast changing too is the cultural flavour and by the time we reached Ngaundere we were into Islamic Africa.

The roads are good from here to Garoua. It was whilst walking round the bustling, muddy market in Garoua that I felt something snatched from my back pocket. I spun round; "Hey!" but didn't know which one of the many faces was responsible. I racked my brain to think what could have been in there, then remembered it was my soap which I'd put in my pocket after washing in a lake that morning! Shortly afterwards in the town I saw another thief get caught and have thirty or forty people chase him through the streets, hitting him with sticks, throwing stones, punches and kicks. The mob was laughing and excited and quickly gathered more eager members. At last he was thrown roughly into a car for his own safety and taken to the police. Chasing thieves is good sport and almost everyone, young and old, appears to want to get in on it.

The night before crossing the border into Nigeria we camped at an idyllic spot with towering granite tors and a small waterfall which it was possible to get behind – a perfect camp shower. During the night I had the most terrifying awakening - a massive explosion not twenty yards from the truck - the shattering reverberations left me quaking in my bed. It was a lightning strike. The thunderstorm continued until morning and we completed our border formalities in the pouring rain.

At the small Nigerian border post I first took our eight passports to immigration and, one by one, the group filed in to complete forms. From the large, stark concrete customs office opposite a voice boomed and echoed.

"Hey, amigo! Hey! Come here."

I walked briskly over to the office in which were four customs officers in military uniforms. The cool, clever dude in the mirror 'shades' ordered me to where he was standing. I could smell he'd been drinking.

"Where is your passport?" he demanded.

"It's in immigration," I replied.

"What is your nationality?"

"British."

"You are a spy!" he accused.

"I am not."

"Yes, you are, you are a spy and I'm refusing you entry into Nigeria."

"I'm not a spy. I'm a driver for this company that takes tourists through Africa."

"Stop that! Stop that!" he interrupted.

He kept mumbling about Margaret Thatcher and South Africa. The others in the office evidently found all this quite amusing and this encouraged him to continue...

"You white guys are all the same; killing black people in South Africa," he snarled, "You'll go back to England and write stories about how bad it is here."

I didn't tell him that he'd already made this very likely.

"You are a spy – what is your purpose here?"

He wasn't intimidating me but I wasn't enjoying his little game. I knew that he didn't really believe me to be a spy and that, if I could hold my own, he would eventually let us in.

Immigration over, he wanted everyone in the office with their bags. He let us wait for half an hour before dealing with us. During this time we were surprised to watch him treat everyone else as badly. His cringing side-kick, Egor, found him most amusing and I could just see him scurrying round stooping, "Yes, master, whatever you say, master!"

The first bag to be searched was full of letters which he read, clothes that he searched, and malaria pills which he threatened to confiscate, also – to my horror – a South African loose-leaf visa!

"Have you been to South Africa?" he demanded of Benny.

"Er, well, yes, at the start of the trip."

I was convinced that that would be it – "Go back to Cameroun, do not pass 'Go', do not collect £200!" – which we couldn't have done anyway as we only had single entry Cameroun visas.

Amazingly enough he let it go and was so bored reading all the letters that he hardly bothered with the rest of the bags and soon we were allowed to leave.

About 10kms down the road I was stopped by a policeman. Three smartly dressed men approached me and I shook their hands as they were introduced as being a police officer, a customs officer, and an immigration officer.

"Your papers have all been dealt with okay?" asked the policeman.

"Yes, yes, fine."

"Are you tourists?"

"That's right."

"You are very welcome in Nigeria, we wish you a safe and enjoyable journey."

"Thank you."

We all shook hands once more and then left, now feeling much happier about being in Nigeria.

The main trunk roads are excellent and we covered the 800kms to Kano in less than two days, only having been given three-day visas for Nigeria in Cameroun. Once in Kano I had first to get all our visas extended and this itself took over a day.

Kano is a fascinating city and a lot of the old mud-walled buildings survive. It has an excellent museum concerned as much with building techniques as with local history. It is a town that in many ways reminded me of Morocco with the large bustling markets, mosques, tiny narrow streets, dye pits and Muslims dressed in white robes and colourful hats. In many Arab countries women are never seen, it's impossible to buy a beer and the result is that many men behave like depraved animals and hassle for alcohol and hound Western women. Here, however, some sort of balance seems to have been struck. Western women, even in shorts, can walk around in relative safety from leering eyes or worse, local women are not hidden away or covered up and still are occasionally bare-breasted. Beer is sold openly and, although I never saw a Muslim drunk, many of them have no objection to an occasional cold beer. Five times a day they must pray; this involves a ritual of washing hands and feet before performing a series of movements and postures. Whatever you may feel about this, it does seem to make them very relaxed and apparently contented. One aspect of this, however, that I do find hard to accept is the practice of cutting thieves' hands off. There are also weekly televised public executions for a range of offences from drug smuggling to armed robbery, although the public executions are not limited to Islamic areas. (There were four armed robberies during my stay in Kano). Unusually for Africa, the police are not dressed up as military personnel and at the many road-blocks they ask where we're from and where we're going and – "Is there a road all that way?" and "We hope you have a safe journey".

Perhaps because there are, at present, very few tourists here, the people are incredibly and genuinely friendly. The usual greeting is "You are welcome" and people stop you in the street to ask where you are from and where you're going, etc. It is very refreshing not to have people trying to hard-sell trinkets or be pestered by begging children. During the week that we spent there we met a group of expatriates who took us out to the 'Flying Club' which is the closest I've come to 'going down to the pub' for a year! We also ended up going to two parties with huge slap-up meals laid on for VSO arrivals. What a contrast to Chad!

I had expected my much needed new piston to be waiting for me at the airport but no ... I telexed London and they said it would be with me in two days. So after two days I went out to the airport to find that no cargo had been loaded onto that plane. There's one a day so I went back next day. It had gone straight to Lagos without stopping. The freight would be brought from there by domestic flight... Next day I found one pallet of cargo from London but nothing for me. It was now Friday and I was told that customs didn't work at weekends. Another Telex confirmed my parcel would arrive at 3.00am on Saturday.

I'd asked Jim to start re-assembling the engine, our visa extensions being due to expire on the Sunday, and decided to send Jim and the group to Agadez in Niger on five cylinders whilst I would stay in Kano, extend my visa, pick up the parts on the Monday and catch them up on local transport. I had to *try* to get my parts on Saturday so I went back to the airport and soon found my parcel in the warehouse.

"Ah, there it is!" I grabbed it.

"The problem is the Customs don't work today, so can't release it! You must also collect freight through an agent". Of course I knew all this, especially after having worked around Heathrow airfreight for a year or so.

"But it's very important, my visa expires, blah, blah, blah," I showed him my passport.

"Hmm, well if you pay 75 Naira (about £15 on the black market or £65 in the bank) for processing the documents and open the package here you can take it."

"Seventy-five! Phew, maybe I'll have to come back on Monday. I'll give you 20N." I opened the box and pulled out a gleaming piston. They were now pretending to calculate how much for processing the paperwork.

"So and so needs ten, and so and so needs five and so and so needs five."

"So that's twenty", I interrupted.

"Give thirty."

"Twenty."

"Okay, twenty-five."

"Good." I pulled out 25N and after carefully concealing the piston, strolled out having managed to by-pass customs and agents and two hours of tedious paperwork.

When I returned to the camp, Jim had just finished the engine. "Okay Jim, let's strip it down again!" The two of us spent the whole day installing our new piston and got it running that night. Next day, early, we left.

It was only a day's drive to the Niger border during which time we met two other overland trucks going south. So it was in the shabby immigration office that all our passport and visa details were entered into a book. At the second to last passport the officer stopped abruptly and rather gleefully pointed out that our Nigerian visas had never been signed by the issuing officer in Douala where we had obtained them. I looked in disbelief. He was right and no-one up to now had noticed.

"You will have to go back to Douala" he said, coldly, "these visas are not valid and have deliberately not been signed."

"But that's impossible, we don't now have visas for Cameroun."

"Then one of you, preferably you, will have to go with all the passports and leave your passengers here."

"But our visas expire today."

"I can extend them for a week."

"How can you extend invalid visas?"

"Go and speak with your friends and decide what you are going to do."

So the options were:- go to the next border post along, after signing the visas ourselves; trouble there was that he'd already given us exit stamps which would have to be cancelled so provoking an enquiry at the next border crossing. Or we could go back down the road on the pretence of going back to Douala, sign the visas and return after a few days, but then we'd have lost the best part of a week. The only practical way out, and we both knew it, was "How much?"

He looked around furtively as he considered my question – and I knew he could more-or-less pick a figure at will.

"Ten dollars?" He almost whispered. Hugely relieved I passed it surreptitiously under the table trying hard not to smile.

The transition from scrubland to desert is remarkably abrupt – only a day's driving, in fact. It was noticeable also, how much sickness there is here, hundreds of blind people or ill children. Niger is one of the countries receiving aid at the moment. There is a high frequency of beggars here and this is something we've seen very little of generally in Africa. I wonder whether a lot of this direct aid makes people expect Westerners to just dole out everything they have on the spot. It does feel like that sometimes. (I do believe, however, that the long term projects, water pumping and purifying schemes, tree planting and agricultural schemes *are* worthwhile).

Agadez... 120°F. Hot wind, like holding a hair-dryer two inches from your face; dehydrating. We spent the afternoons drinking 'tea' with Tuareg nomads. Their tea is made very strong with Chinese green tea and mint. It is drunk from small glasses with about two dessert spoons of sugar. I enjoyed it to start with but on day three I overdosed on sugar and went to bed feeling sick.

I asked a lad if it was possible to visit the mosque. He said it was and so at 8.30am we walked down to the 'Palace'. We apparently had to first obtain permission from the Sultan before we could enter the mosque. Poor timing! The German

Ambassador was with him for about two hours. No-one minds sitting in the shade for about two hours here, though. What else can you do in this heat?

So we sat in the archway and shook hands with the people passing through. Tall, elegant men in flowing white robes, faces covered from the sun by their sheshes (a kind of turban made of either pale green, white, red, black or indigo woven cotton, some being fifteen metres in length). Old men with wooden legs, sinister men in black sheshes with piercing white eyes, old women chatting to us in unintelligible language and a large crowd of children parading the streets with drums and spears and flags.

At length the German Ambassador left and the Sultan emerged to recline on a comfortable deck-chair in the courtyard. We were beckoned in and shook hands with him after being careful to remove our shoes. He seemed like a kind man, pleased to help and happy for us to visit the mosque. We thanked him very much and bowed and scraped out of the gate towards the mosque.

Agadez mosque is an old and fascinating construction dating back to the fourteenth or fifteenth century. It is like a tall, narrow pyramid with sticks bristling out all the way to the small, walled platform at the top. The view of the town was superb and enabled us to pick out other points of interest to visit, such as the Tuareg camel market.

Ah yes... the Tuareg camel market... Two Germans of about my age arrived at the campsite in a Land Rover, they'd been out to the Tuareg market and asked about joining a genuine Tuareg salt caravan. Sure enough, a caravan would be leaving for the Aïr mountains in two days and they wouldn't have to pay but would be expected to trade sugar, salt and chewing tobacco with the nomads for water and use of the camels, etc. They could also leave their Land Rover in the small yard behind the 'Hotel Sahara'.

Next day they spent 300 French francs (about £30) on sugar, salt and tobacco at the Tuareg market and the following morning drove to the Hotel Sahara to park their car. But what's this? Nowhere to put the Land Rover? And what, no caravan? I'm not sure where the laughter was loudest, amongst the other campers or the Tuareg traders!

Assamakka is a desolate outpost at a small oasis in a calm ocean of sand. Calm today but only two weeks ago a storm levelled the customs and immigration huts and many of the temporary nomadic and semi-permanent dwellings around. Passports had been scattered in the wilderness and the army had apparently been called in to look for them and other documents. Gladly the bar – the last bar until Spain – had survived so we had the last beer for a long time after completing border formalities and headed off towards Ain Guezzam, the Algerian entry post. There is 30km of poorly marked piste between the two border posts which is notoriously difficult. Several people a year have been known to go missing here. Luckily we had little trouble and we are now travelling together with James and Judy, the couple with the Land Rover we first met in Kisangani. It is quite reassuring to have two vehicles sometimes.

Algerian formalities were no problem as it turned out we'd met the officials in the bar a few hours earlier! We left Ain Guezzam on the scorching bleach following four-foot posts at 5km intervals. Sometimes we are following piles of stones every hundred metres or so, stretching straight across a horizontal haze; an enigma for some future age.

Then... no markers at all, just a maze of tyre tracks in the soft sand. Follow a track, yes, this looks okay, till "hmm, only one set of tracks left - where did everyone else go?" Then it's stand on the roof with the compass and binoculars to find a wreck, maybe, an old tyre, a truck, or it's turn around and follow your own tracks back to where you were before you became uncertain.

The number of wrecked vehicles is quite worrying; there are hundreds. Of course they do not deteriorate in this climate, instead they become sand-blasted and are often a smart gun-metal grey. On the Algerian border we met some people travelling south in cars. They had found two Germans with a VW Combi van lost and broken down 5km from the piste. They had taken them on board and left yet another piece of desert furniture, first to the mechanical scavengers and then to the sand, the wind and the sun. I often wonder how many of the other vehicle owners were not so lucky.

We have now arrived at Tamanrasset and I have got your letter. I never did get the one addressed to Bangui. Several other people were letters short there. I left a note for the driver following me to send it back home. I read your letter in the bank whilst we were all changing our compulsory £150. Regarding your strong words over my poem about the people of Botswana, I wasn't really sneering but the contrast in lifestyles was so marked I only wanted to highlight it. Enough said.

Anyway, I'm due back on the 20/21 October so I'll see you as soon after that as Exodus will allow.

Love,
Graham.

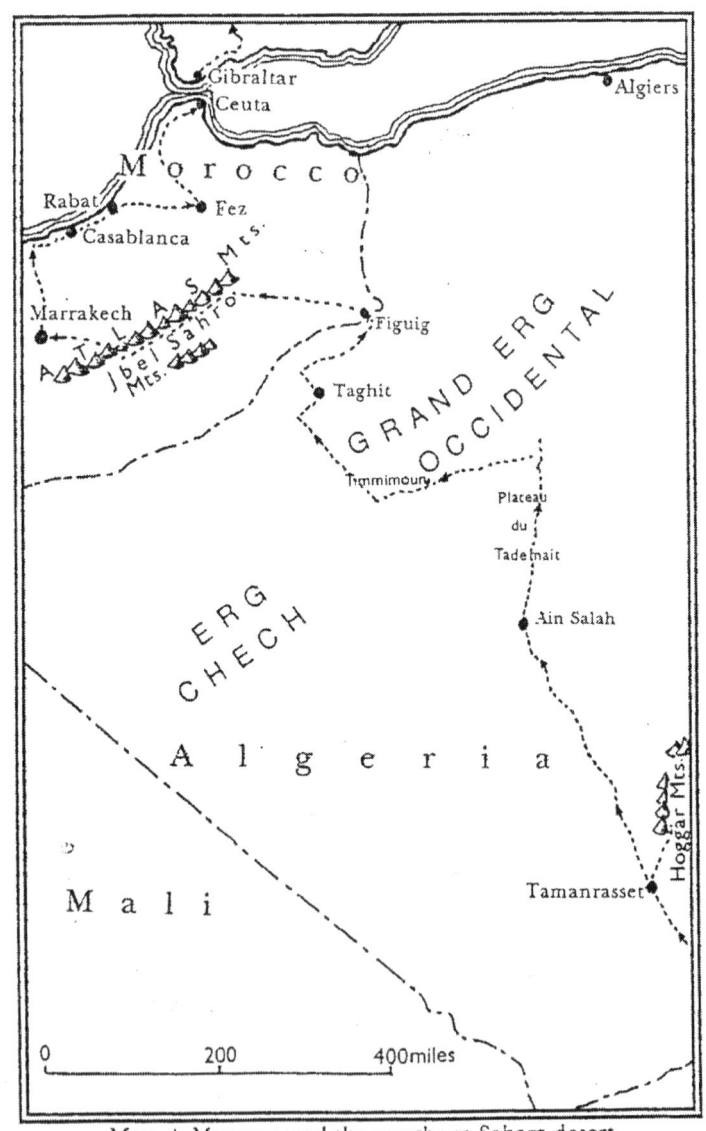

Map 4b. Morocco and the northern Sahara desert.

100km North of Ain Salah
Sahara Desert, Algeria
27 September 1986

Dear All

We're still in the heart of the desert. I thought I'd seen flat plains before, but when I saw this one I realised I had not. There is nothing for many times further than the eye can see. Only flat grey stones on amber sand.
BREATHTAKING VIEW!
I turn my head all about and see the same sharp severe horizon cutting the world in two...
SSHHLEW!
The third dimension is excluded and missing.
A flat blue and grey sandwich.
A living photograph of a calm ocean.
There is nothing happening here and nothing is about to happen.
I feel close to nothing and perfection; although nowhere can be described in absolute terms, this is very nearly nowhere and a perfect flat plain, violated only by the vehicle tracks, like obscene graffiti, laid across it.

The rest of Algeria passed without incident except that we lost another member of the group; Wolfgang, our middle-aged German friend. He'd not been too happy since entering the desert; he lives in Australia so felt that he'd seen enough of all that. He was also missing his wife, Ingrid, who'd been with us from Nairobi to Bangui. It was in Timmimoun, Algeria, that he met two young Germans with a truck who were going straight back to Europe. They were only too pleased to have him pay a third of the expenses.

The night before we left Algeria for Morocco, I warned the group that "This border crossing is potentially the worst in Africa"; I asked them to dress smart for the occasion and to be prepared for hours of hassles and waiting.

This, the Beni-Ounif to Figuig crossing, so far held the record for my longest ever of fifteen hours. On top of this the southbound truck we'd recently met said that one of the Algerian customs officers had asked one of the women in the group to be strip-searched. She assumed that she must comply so, she started taking her clothes off behind the filing cabinet as ordered. It was only when he tried to kiss her that she realised her mistake and raised the alarm. After that the driver made

sure he was present with the customs officer (who was only entitled to turn out pockets at the most). (I was to learn later that at about the same time of our crossing, this driver, who we'd spent some time with on the Nigerian-Niger border, had tragically died of malaria in Cameroun). Much to everyone's surprise it took only an hour to pass Algerian exit formalities and it didn't even cost us any whisky, which can be sold for up to £60.00 a bottle here.

In order to enter Morocco with a large vehicle, it is necessary to have a telex waiting at the border from the Moroccan authorities, previously arranged through the British Embassy, authorising the vehicle's entry. I'd given Exodus all the necessary details in Kano, Nigeria, stating that I expected to arrive on the 5th October. In Timmimoun I realised that I'd be arriving instead on the 2nd, so I'd telexed again and told them the earlier date. They replied that it should be okay but that it was now out of their hands in any case. So we pulled up to the Moroccan barrier between rugged mountains amongst the date palms. I walked up to the tent that is the customs and immigration office, bid them "Bonjour" and was sat down whilst they telephoned town to find my telex.

"It's not there" he eventually said. "Maybe it's at Oujda." Oujda is the only other crossing 400km north. They'd phone from town, he said, and ring back with the verdict.

Meanwhile, we waited... I was fed handfuls of delicious dates and glasses of sweet mint tea (much more palatable than the Tuareg tea) until eventually the phone rang... No telex at Oujda. I explained that we were to have arrived on the 5th and perhaps it hadn't yet been sent.

"You have two choices," he said calmly. "Either you go back to Algeria or go to Figuig town on foot to contact your Embassy." The first wasn't a choice as it would have meant changing another obligatory 1000.00 Dinars (£150) each! I walked into town and had to report to the police for my passport stamp. I'd taken along Carol, one of my group who speaks fluent French. The policeman looked at our passports.

"You'll have to come with me to the hospital", he said and beckoned us to follow as he strode out into the street.

"The hospital?" We puzzled; perhaps the chief of police was ill and had to stamp our passports from his bed; or maybe the officer in charge of passports doubles as a part-time doctor. We were led into a small hospital and immediately asked our names and weights before being pushed towards a room with a large sign on the door – 'INJECTIONS'.

"Wait a minute," we protested. "We have these certificates to prove we've been vaccinated against cholera, yellow fever and typhoid; they've been good enough right through Africa." The doctor wasn't impressed; we asked to see someone more senior who was also unimpressed. He eventually conceded that we'd have to take some tablets instead which were a cholera preventative as there was cholera in Algeria.

It's true that there is cholera in some parts of Algeria; it's also true that the vaccination is almost useless, but to take so-called preventative tablets after leaving Algeria was obviously no good either. We were given three large tablets each for which we had to sign and were issued with a certificate. It was now 11.40am and the banks and post office would close at 12.00. The senior policeman back at the police station browsed slowly through our passports and at 4 minutes to twelve strolled out of his office to demand;

"Baggage!"

We explained our story *again* and stressed the urgency as we had to phone Rabat. He gave us our passports and said we could change money at the Post Office.

As we expected, at the Post Office we were told that we'd have to go to the Bank to change money; so we had to wait until 3.00pm when everything re-opened after siesta. A local guy of about my age, who worked in a hotel, kindly fed us on credit.

At 3.00pm I changed some money and spent two hours in the Post Office waiting for my call to Rabat. There is only one phone and the only man allowed to use it has also to deal with everything else single-handed in this busy Post Office. He's actually quite efficient but it's all stacked against him. In the end I gave up and went back to the small hotel on the way out of town, where we'd had lunch and asked the owner, also the owner of the petrol station downstairs, if I could use his phone. After four or five attempts I got through to the British Embassy:

"No, we have no information whatsoever about your vehicle" (What!?)

"I'll give you it now; my name is Graham Burgess and...'CLICK'...It's gone dead!"

"Oh yes," said the owner, "You're only allowed a short time then it cuts off."

"Terrific, can I try again?"

"No, that's it for a long time."

It was now almost 5.30pm so it wasn't worth doing any more as the Embassy would be closing. I just hoped that the woman I'd spoken to had the presence of mind to telex Exodus the following morning.

The guards at the border were friendly enough; we did supply one of them with bits of our firewood for a table he was making. Another wanted a drop of whisky, but I think we were an interesting distraction for them. It looked like we were going to be around for at least four days as the weekend was coming up, so I suggested to the group that they take local transport and we'd meet up with them once we'd got the truck through.

The following day I spent all morning in the Post Office to no avail. "It seems there's something wrong with the lines!" The hotel phone was dead all day. Another siesta in a cafe drinking mint tea, then back for the afternoon shift in the Post Office after waving goodbye to three of the group who've caught a bus.

"And then there were four!

At about 4.15pm I got through to the Embassy. It turned out that there is an Exodus truck southbound with twenty passengers stuck at Ceuta with the same problem. Obviously someone somewhere has omitted to do some paperwork! This leaves us to sit in no-man's-land all weekend and hope the telex turns up on Monday.

Saturday, shift change at the border and we get a miserable officer who doesn't want us around so, after changing a broken spring, we left the truck and booked into a seedy hotel up the road; and that's where I am now.

It ultimately took us a week to get our authorisation through and after meeting up with our passengers, we headed straight for Marrakech. Predictably enough we met the southbound truck and swapped stories whilst on our two-day Atlas Mountain trek. We also found that non-EEC travellers now need visas to enter France - just when I thought we'd finished with all that! So we had to go to Rabat, the capital, to buy them for our Aussies and Kiwis. Unfortunately Moroccans now need French visas as well and it seemed as though they'd all decided to apply at the same time, either out of spite for their now being required, or just in case they should decide to go there. We waited all day in a queue which quickly dissolved into a rabble of three or four hundred people pushing and shouting and fighting outside the French Embassy's newly opened annex. We eventually gave up, having got nowhere after five hours.

About 100km out of Rabat on the road to Fez, our engine started making a loud 'clacking' noise. Now all you folks back there in England probably think Morocco is a long way away but, believe me, to us it's nearly home! The noise got steadily worse over the following two days to the ferry at Ceuta. So bad, in fact, that I decided to forego the spectacular mountain route in favour of the easier main road.

Whilst waiting in the queue of vehicles about to board the boat to Spain, I suddenly couldn't get out of first gear, not even into neutral. When the queue eventually moved I had to re-start the engine with my foot on the clutch and scream along at a dead-slow crawl, holding everyone up, belching thick black smoke – which, by now, had got quite bad – and cringing at the awful mechanical noises emanating from beneath the cab.

"You *will* leave Africa," I warned the truck as one might warn a stubborn child not wanting to go home.

We got the French visas in Madrid with no fuss and struck out towards Pamplona. Through various tunnels on these fast main roads, I got our Hazard Warning Triangle ready. Cars overtaking us were now emerging from a cloud of oily black smoke, their drivers shaking their fists or blaring horns angrily.

"Only two more days, baby, you can do it!" I coaxed. Now I could see that all these cars were also sprayed with oil. We stopped and peeped apprehensively under the cab. The engine was hot and dripping with engine oil. The entire underside was also dripping as was the back of the truck. There was, needless to say, not much oil left in the engine. I did have a pretty good idea what had gone wrong, having seen similar symptoms twice before. I was proved right after reluctantly embarking on the engine stripdown I'd been hoping to avoid; number six piston holed, the one opposite the last one that went. So once again, on five cylinders, we chugged through the Pyrenees and France to Le Havre and so to Portsmouth, arriving on the 27th October 1986.

Back at the workshop in Wiltshire I parked the truck and was free to go home for a holiday. I heard later that the next day Terry, the mechanic, had tried to move it but it wouldn't start. Thinking it must have a flat battery he'd put jump leads on it but it still wouldn't turn, so they towed it with the tractor and the rear wheels just dragged on the concrete. The engine had completely seized up. Perfect timing!

After my previous African Christmas, Christmas in UK was a dreary affair. I felt oppressed by the commercialism and depressed by the lifeless and dour singing at the carol service I attended. Oh England – whatever happened to you?

Corrugated piste – mid-Sahara

'Australia' Rock, mid Sahara – with Australian!

The Grand Erg Occidental -1000 miles of sand dunes

Stuck!

Regular Duties

Locally-made vehicles (Zaire)

Self-made toys

The whisky tastes okay if you've got nothing to compare it with!

Found this in Nigeria

Typical public transport

Typical public transport

From Nigeria

Dhow on the Tanzanian coast

Victoria Falls with rainbow. (On full Moons there are Moonbows that look very much like this monochrome photograph).

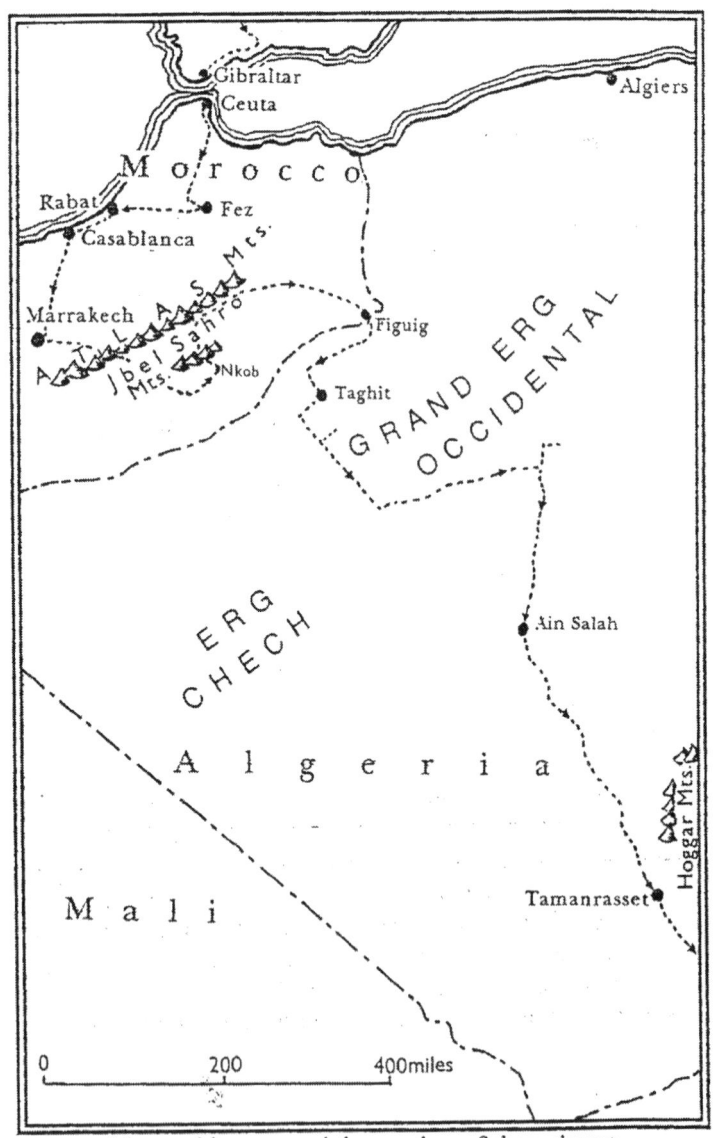

Map 4c. Morocco and the northern Sahara desert.

Rabat, Morocco.
18th February, 1987

Dear All

No doubt you are, by now, waiting for this letter to pop through the door. As usual I've found it hard to get the time to write, and when I do find half-an-hour all I want to do is relax or sleep.

Well, I still haven't decided the form these letters are to take but I did write a piece for the first letter whilst in the workshop, so I thought it would be best to start our adventure right at the beginning; that is in the 'Exodus Expeditions' workshop – a ghastly eyesore set amongst the picturesque thatched cottages of Collingbourne Ducis in Wiltshire.

I returned to work after a welcome two-month break, on 5th January 1987, to find a completely dismembered truck. A chassis propped up on four oil drums, the body on four more and the cab sitting on the floor behind the engine. We had one month to complete the assembly. To help Terry, the full-time mechanic, and myself, there are two trainee drivers, one of whom is likely to be coming with me on February 6th. It's largely my choice as to which one it will be.

Assembly has gone well; I've enjoyed the work and the weekends are soon upon us once again. What a nice change it is to work nine-to-five, five days a week! Each job I've tackled, each piece I've made, I've completed to my satisfaction and I feel good about the vehicle as a result. This has inevitably taken more time than would normally be expected in the workshop where, all too often, jobs are performed carelessly and then only to basic requirements. I have taken to working often late into the night when it's quiet and I can take my time. I spent several hours making a new exhaust pipe, carefully welding each joint, measuring accurately, devising new methods of support to allow flexibility. Terry had walked past and caught me studying it.

"Hah! It's a work of art," he joked. But that's exactly what it was. It's surely what 'craftsmanship' is all about; work undertaken as art, with care and love and followed by a feeling of immense satisfaction upon completion. I suppose I was looking for a feeling for this in the two trainees and after three weeks they'd both shown their attitudes sufficiently for me to make up my mind as to which one will be my co-driver.

Keith had had a fair mechanical background; worked for a while servicing racing motorcycle cylinder heads, then on oil rigs. The trouble is that he's lazy; if he finishes a particular job he'll stop work altogether until someone notices and finds him something else to do. If he comes up against a problem he's stumped, or at least won't apply himself to do it, simply telling others who are usually busy, that he's stuck. He's lazy in his work as well; he'll not use a hacksaw when he can use an oxy-acetylene cutter; a file when there's an angle grinder handy; and who needs spanners when you can use the compressed air hammer drill? In three weeks I have to say that I haven't seen him turn out anything worthwhile, though what annoys me is that his lack of care extends to leaving pools of tools everywhere he's worked – that tend to remain for days afterwards.

Sam, 27 and Swiss, is the alternative. He's had less mechanical experience than Keith but what he lacks in knowledge he makes up for in enthusiasm and a will to learn. He'd been painting for over a week, a mindless task, but when I gave him the job of installing shelves in the cab he took to it eagerly and said he liked to puzzle out problems. He seems to like to see a job done well and tools cleared away when he's finished. I think Sam could do okay in this job. I think Keith will be lucky if he's still employed at the end of his training trip.

Now, perhaps I'm seen as a bit of an 'intrepid explorer' but I think it's important for people to know that before I left on any of my trips, whether it was walking the South West coast path, cycling around Ireland or Europe, I've been SCARED! Scared of what? - of the possibilities; of the unknown. I believe it's important to overcome this fear because it prevents many people from making the changes that perhaps ought to be made. But it's very hard to overcome and this prevents people travelling, moving house or changing their job. Security is not the haven from fear that many think it is but often the instigator of it.

On the 6th February 1987 we left Portsmouth for Le Havre and drove to Paris to pick up the remainder of my group. We had to camp there and I needn't tell you that it was *bloody freezing*! The next day, twenty miles outside Paris, we broke down. Okay, nothing serious, just air in the fuel. Another ten miles and we broke down again, same problem. And again, and again – until we found that we'd sucked in a lump of dirt from the fuel tank into the pipe and blocked it. I made a makeshift filter out of an old sock and it's been as good as gold ever since.

In Spain I followed a minor road to avoid Madrid; it was through a beautiful mountainous area but no-one was really interested; they just wanted to get to Africa. One night we got caught up in a blizzard and had to stay in a small Spanish bar (no-one complained about *that*!).

So, quickly, before we get to Africa, here is a rundown of the group:

Jonas. Norwegian engineer. Always wears big boots and lots of clothes. He's fit and runs every day. Has a little goatee beard and no moustache. He's quiet but speaks English well.

Cynthia. Australian travel agent. She won her place in a competition. She's good fun but has had a serious alcohol problem in the recent past.

Sophia. Danish student. Lively, well-travelled and speaks excellent English.

Philippa. English student. Very English and girlish, apt to be a bit bitchy.

Emma. Friend of Philippa – same.

Viktor. Danish student (Doctor). Half Nigerian, easy-going. Nice guy.

Ida. Danish teacher. Very cheerful and 'cuddly', also the first to get infested with body lice!

Michelle. English, office clerk. Very quiet but also very sharp-witted.

Freja. Danish carpenter. Her English isn't too good so she's very quiet indeed.

Karl. Danish carpenter – Freja's boyfriend, six-foot three and outspoken. I have to be careful not to upset him. He did attempt to 'help me out' during a hassle at a campsite by flooring the owner.

Anna. Danish secretary. Quiet and pleasant, already teamed up with Dr. Viktor.

Ella and Oliver. Older married Danish couple, teachers. Fit, energetic and good members of the group.

Alan. Older Scotsman. Botanist. Very interesting to talk to, gets on well with everyone.

Mats. Swedish student doctor. A bit of a comic. Speaks excellent English and is actively encouraging the other Scandinavians to speak English to avoid a split in the group.

Martine. French student. Has been a problem, stubborn, lazy, immature, but seems to be getting better. Unfortunately, she has all but blown her chances with the others. Time will tell.
Marcus. Danish student. Lazy and sometimes a bit fiery.
Carol. Canadian student. Energetic, go-for-it attitude. Should do okay.
Mille. Danish carpenter. Speaks little English, very withdrawn from the group.
Katrine. Danish student. Lively, excellent English, good fun.
[NOTE: Some names have been changed]

As I mentioned, we had a bit of a hassle at Ceuta campsite when the Spanish owner wanted me to pay in the morning after refusing to accept that I'd already paid him the previous evening. When I tried to reason with him he (and his alsatian dog) became alarmingly aggressive and in the commotion, 'The Boys' appeared armed with baseball bats and he with a revolver (after Karl had sent him sprawling in the dust). I paid twice but it was a bit worrying for a moment.

Then we were in Morocco and, soon enough, in Fez. As we drove into town a car pulled up alongside.

"You know Ghali?" asked the driver. Well, I was actually hoping to avoid him but I knew that would not be easy. He's virtually the 'Godfather' of Fez. I said we wanted to go to the Hamman (Turkish Baths) first so he led us there. It turned out that he's attempting to work independently of Ghali! He seemed okay so I agreed that he'd be our guide the following day. He asked me out for a drink and I accepted, provided that we got the camp sorted out first.

At the campsite a big black limo slowly drove through the gates. Our guide looked a little nervous as he hurriedly said:

"Look, these are Ghali's men. Just tell them that you're all fixed up already."

Three 'Bugsy Malones' waddled up, reeking of alcohol.

"We're from Ghali," they said. "We'll be your guides tomorrow."

"Er, well, I've got everything sorted out already, actually."

"Who with?"

"This chap here – oh, where's he gone?" Our friend was lurking in the shadows. The big man, Ghali's brother as it turned out, waddled a step closer.

"I don't think you understand the way things *work* here in Morocco."

"Well, this puts me in a difficult position. Why don't you talk it over with this guy and let me know what you decide." The first man reappeared nervously. They talked briefly and he then informed me that Ghali's brother would be our guide after all.

The three 'gangsters' then asked me out for the obligatory drink and said they'd pick me up at 9.00pm. Meanwhile I consumed as much mashed potato and milk as possible. I remember what state Jim came back in last time.

As expected, after meeting Ghali himself in the hotel bar along with several of the businessmen he's got in his pocket, the evening steadily blurred, even for Sam who doesn't drink except for an occasional wine. When Ghali buys the drinks it's whisky and he won't take no for an answer. It's a symbol of his influence – alcohol being somewhat scarce here. The evening blurred from the hotel to the night-club and on to the late-night cafe (owned by Ghali). I enjoyed myself but was horrified the next morning when Sam reminded me that I'd eaten sheep's head, eyes and all. And I'm a vegetarian!

The tour went well the next day and Ghali's brother turned out to be a fairly good guide. I even stomached the tannery where the sheep's heads were piled high and stinking. The inevitable carpet warehouse experience lasted three-and-a-half hours and I was almost asleep by the end after only two hours sleep in the night. I think they were a little disappointed that only three people bought carpets. I'd put them off a bit because I dislike the whole scene. Even so, I got about £100 commission which makes you wonder how much *they* get. The women who make them are allegedly paid peanuts, even though it's supposed to be a co-operative.

Fez Medina (or old town) doesn't lose its impact on subsequent visits - a maze of narrow passageways and a hive of every activity you can imagine. We had to go to Rabat again for Central African visas, which was a nice break. Rabat is far more relaxed and no hassle at all compared to Fez. Next we arrived in Marrakech, now hot and sunny, amongst the palm trees. I spent much of our two days here in the main square. I concealed my tape recorder and microphone and went around the ever-changing array of street entertainers: bands, acrobats, snake charmers, monkey circus, dove circus, some guy with scorpions on his face who killed small birds, blind lute players, plays, storytellers, blind beggars chanting "Allah" ... "Allah", violinists, etc., etc., etc. I managed to record quite a lot despite having the 'pause' button pushed for two hours...

Perhaps the sight that sticks most firmly in my mind was that of a middle-aged German man, dressed in dazzling white T-shirt and shorts pointing his video camera at a crumpled blind man of about the same age, in ragged clothes under a battered umbrella with his two children, and playing his violin whilst singing a very moving song. Each song earned maybe sixty or seventy centimes (about 5p) which he gathered up with groping, fumbling fingers, to give to his children.

It's now a long time since I last added to this letter. It's been hard to find the time or the inspiration I'm afraid. I think the novel will have to wait awhile. It seems as though every day that passes provides another opportunity for a complete short story but, like dreams, they seem to slip away, perhaps to be recalled one day but, for the moment, gone. The group have all gone up to the Hoggar Mountains leaving me in blissful solitude in Tammanrasset campsite. There are a lot of other cross-desert travellers here, most of them intending to sell their vehicles in Niger. There are even a few cyclists here. I'll see what I remember from the last two weeks.

The first thing I wanted to write about was the unbelievable hospitality we found in Morocco. Even after having been there twice before, it was a surprise. We'd camped at the municipal campsite in Salé, the old town on the opposite bank of the estuary to Rabat.

Two of the group had predictably acquired a 'guide', and he had, apparently, invited all of us to his house for a meal, provided we bought the food. Now, I'm being very careful not to become cynical, but I've met too many Moroccans who are just after my money in one way or another. I even met a Moroccan who advised me to 'Never trust a Moroccan' and made it clear he included himself!

This lesson can be an expensive one on your first visit, which is why it's important to always tell these 'guides' that you've been to Morocco before, even if you haven't – it makes them a bit more wary that you'll know their tricks. Anyway, the food - couscous, chicken and vegetables - was duly bought and taken back to the small house, lost deep in the maze of the Medina, to be prepared by the women of the house. At 8pm we were met at the campsite by Mustafa and Mohammed, who led us through the narrow streets and, at length, we were shown into an upstairs room furnished in traditional Moroccan style, although much poorer and less lavish than the traditional houses I've previously visited. The men of the house, plus friends, introduced themselves and we talked or listened or looked around at our surroundings. In Moroccan houses, traditionally, there is one room that is often long and narrow which has covered bench seats all around the walls with low tables in the middle. Carpets or rugs are spread on the floor. The windows have no glass but ornate iron grilles with internal shutters for night-time. If the family has money, rugs with intricate designs and elaborate curtains cover the walls. This room, which, apart from a cramped and dingy kitchen where the women-folk spent their time, was the only room the family had and the walls peeled bare blue distemper. The family itself consisted of four children, their mother, her sister and her thirty year old son, Mustafa; grandmother, and the children's father's brother (father is in prison), a woman whom they took in as she had no family and another man who is a friend.

The couscous arrived. Three huge plates, one for each table, piled high with food, topped with vegetables and pieces of chicken. As is the tradition in Morocco, all on each table eat from the same plate with the fingers. It's okay and water is always provided to wash your hands. After eating, a tape-player was produced and soon we were all dancing to the distorted wailing and Arabic beat. It was a very enjoyable evening, the family asked for nothing more than a share of the food.

It had been too cold to go trekking in the High Atlas so, on the advice of Alan, the workshop manager who's just done a season's trekking here, we drove over the Atlas and down south of Ouarazazate. Once over the pass of Tizi-n-Tichka we found ourselves immediately in the Sahara – the contrast always astonishing. It felt good to be in the desert once again. It does have a strange attraction; all that space. It has that same feeling of excitement as the morning after a blizzard when you wake up to find your town has been cut off. Nature taken to the extreme, having got the better of mankind.

We drove to the southern side of the 'Jbel Sahro' mountain range to a place called Nkob where, with the assistance of a very sketchy sketch map, I turned left down a rough track towards the mountains. The track eventually petered out near three buildings. There were a few people around so I stopped and asked one of the men if we could camp on the flat area by his house as the whole of the rest of the area was strewn with rocks. He was delighted and, once we'd put up the tents, he insisted we join him for a cup of mint tea. The bare mountains rose pink from the lifeless, stony, lunar waste in the setting sunlight as we entered the squat concrete and mud building. Through the door, a high corridor, then through another and you could almost hear the strumming of the harps as we entered a lush courtyard with painted white and green colonnades, a fountain and orange trees heavy with fruit. Across the courtyard we were led into a room such as I've previously described – long with plush, covered bench seats, rich and ornate. The mint tea was brought and, with much ceremony, not to mention sugar, poured expertly from a great height into each glass. During tea our host, Ben Youssef, invited us to eat couscous with them that evening. I thought I'd better refuse, we being twenty in number (two are still in Rabat getting visas). He insisted there was 'no problem' so I accepted. We all washed and changed for dinner; couscous topped with lentils and spices served, as before, on huge plates, each between five people. There was so much that only my table could finish (I can't bear to see food wasted – though I don't know how this squares with Moroccan custom). More mint tea and talking followed. Ben Youssef, it emerged, had himself done a fair amount of travelling – in Europe and North America. He worked for eleven months of the year in Marrakech, in a bank. The other month is either spent here or travelling. Here he lives with his brothers and their families. As before, the women are not seen. They just cook the food and eat in the kitchen with the children.

Next day, early, we set off to hike into the mountains. It was a thoroughly enjoyable day and I'm glad to find I have an energetic group. That evening we were once again invited to mint tea and, once again, to couscous. I told him we were concerned not to eat all his food but he insisted that it was no problem and made it clear he'd be offended if we refused, so again it was that we knelt down to couscous, this time with vegetables and goat meat on top. When we left the following day Ben Youssef's brother gave us some flowers that had been carefully made from wire and wool. We gave them our addresses and sincere gratitude, but somehow financial reward seemed inappropriate even here in Morocco, though I made it plain that it was available should he wish to take it. Ben Youssef had given us the sort of traditional hospitality that could be found world-wide before the advent of tourism, terrorism and commercialism, for we really were the first tourists here. May I one day get the chance to provide such hospitality myself.

When Alan, in the workshop, had said that the road between Nkob and Iknion (which is not on my map) was good, I asked him if it was better than the road between the Todra and Dades gorges, which I'd attempted last year before giving up out of concern for our safety on that narrow mountain track.

"Huh, you didn't go up there did you?" he said. "No, it's much better than that." I just found myself wondering sometimes whether the donkey he rode up here was eight feet wide and weighed twelve tons! It certainly was a bit hairy at times. We descended steeply into a gorge on a rocky track with a deep chasm to our right. The passengers in the cab had their hands over their faces just peeping through their fingers like it was some horror film. At one point there had been a bit of a landslide and there was a pile of earth on the track. Well, it was either stop and dig it all away or drive over it. It was only on one side of the road so I knew it could make the truck lean over quite a bit, though I also judged it to be well within the vehicle's capabilities. Slowly I drove over the pile and the truck leaned over towards the drop.

Screams and whimpers wafted in from the back as many of the group were convinced we were on our way down. I remember a story from another driver who'd ended up on a similar road, gone round a sharp bend and seen one of his group leap from the safari seat, roll like a karate expert, and end up on his feet, convinced the truck would go over the edge. The driver stopped, amazed, to pick him up. Luckily my group had more confidence than *that!*

Once we'd reached the valley bottom, we crawled slowly over stony, dry river beds, surprising the occasional local and damaging bridges. Before the Big Ascent of the mountain range (the pass is at 2,200m) I stopped and apprehensively scanned the zigzagging road with my binoculars. Perhaps I was looking for an obvious obstruction so that I wouldn't have to go through with it. The group were more worried about the possibility of going *back*. So, onward and upward. The road is hideously rocky and steep, though thankfully it appeared to be strong enough. Second gear, low ratio, grinding, climbing stairs on all fours, lurching violently, twisting, turning higher and higher. The landscape is unreal. Massive rounded pillars over there and black jagged columns here, smooth stony hills and soaring craggy mountains; and no vegetation, no signs of any life except for this 'road'. Now a rather tight hair-pin bend - oh-no, the truck won't get round. So I have to shunt back twice with the back of the truck overhanging the precipice to get around and again on the next and the next – six times in all. It's not my favourite manoeuvre at all but it all went okay and when we eventually got to the top we stopped for lunch. My hands were sore from gripping the steering wheel which had tried to snatch itself free on each rock we climbed over (these trucks don't have power steering). I now noticed that we had a broken main leaf on one of our rear springs so we had an extended lunch whilst some volunteers helped me to change it. I was a little worried that the road down the other side would be as bad but, to my relief, it was a great improvement and soon we were cruising across the wide plains toward Todra Gorge.

The guys who run the cafe at Todra immediately recognised me and invited me to eat 'Tajine' with them. Once again, one plate between five, this time eating with lumps of fresh bread. After mint tea I got a free bedroom where I had a very well-needed sleep.

The border at Figuig held no fear for me, having spent a week there last year. I was even looking forward to seeing some familiar faces. I did; two policemen stopped me as I drove into town.

"You must report to the Police Station," one said.

"I know," I said, "I've been here before."

"I remember you," the policeman smiled.

The police station didn't open until 9.00am, one hour, so we filled the water tank and had a coffee. By the time we returned, the two policemen were sitting outside.

"Well," they started, "it's Sunday and the Chief's asleep. If you give us a bottle of whisky we'll go and get him, otherwise you'll have to wait until tomorrow."

I gave him one of my miniature bottles and he laughed. It's the 26th anniversary of the King's inauguration on 3rd March so these guys want to celebrate! I eventually gave in and gave them a half-bottle of Johnnie Walkers. They went to find the Chief. I instantly recognised him and he me. He was very easy on us and only bothered searching, till he found the other bottle of whisky.

"Ah you have whisky!" he said.

"Only one bottle," I admitted. He checked everyone's passport and gave them all back one at a time, making a great play of attempting to pronounce each name. One-by-one the group went back to the truck. My passport was last. Now alone with him in the police station he asked me for the whisky. I told him I needed it to sell in Algeria for my pocket money but it made no impression. He put my passport in his drawer saying that when he had the whisky I would have my passport. I was now really annoyed but all the same had to hand it over with a smile and a "Bon Fête" and perhaps a "hope you choke on it" under my breath.

Luckily customs officers didn't ask for anything and although the immigration officers at the border did, they didn't push it so didn't get anything. Algerian formalities went slowly but without problems, the whole crossing being done, for me, in the record time of nine hours.

Since my brief description of the group things have, of course, developed further, though so far there's been no serious Danish/everyone else split, which is a danger, there being eleven of them speaking to each other in Danish. They certainly can be a handful, though; I drive for six hours over rocks and soft sand till I've had enough, then jump out of the cab to be faced by 'twenty questions', lost tent-pegs and broken padlock keys! I thought I'd got rid of them for tonight but they all came back halfway through this letter when the owner of the refuge in the

Hoggar mountains had tried to charge them an extra 80 dinars (£11.50) for camel-meat soup and rice, a 'continental breakfast' and a few square feet of floor space to sleep on, when they'd already paid 240 dinars each. Oh well - I've retreated to the cab and am not going to let anyone disturb my peace tonight.

It's morning now and strange to hear the Algerian brass band practising here in the Sahara desert; not much African spontaneity there, disciplined music, disciplined men. It did, however, bring back fond childhood memories of when a local brass band near Bradford, Yorkshire would play in the street on Sundays. I wonder if they still do?

Thanks to those of you who sent letters and birthday cards which I received yesterday. I should be in Agadez on the 13th March. I'll close now before this letter gets any thicker (thick letters get opened!).

All the best,
Love,
Graham.

Between Assamakka and Arlit
Niger
12th March 1987

Dear All.

I'm writing this on what will be our last night in the desert, all being well. We left Tamanrasset three days ago to cross the desert, for it is not until you head south from there that you lose the security of a road and regular water points. It is 400km of difficult piste to Assamakka, the tiny oasis that is the Niger border post. For some time it is fairly well marked by 4ft posts at 5km intervals but several are fallen or missing. There are also many tracks going off to elsewhere, or more often, to nowhere, that are easy to end up on by mistake. We followed one track for over 30km; it looked fairly good but then deteriorated badly into large troughs of deep soft sand. Three Peugeots came the other way and stopped. There were about six French people with the cars who said that they followed this piste for another 100km. It was very difficult indeed and all other tyre tracks ran out. It ended, they said, at the edge of a vast white plain which they could not even find on their map, and would anyway have meant driving down a rocky escarpment to reach it. They had turned around and advised us to do likewise, which we did. Just a bit further on we could see another Frenchman hopelessly stuck and alone with his car; we pushed him out and he roared off without a word of thanks. We heard later that he had been travelling in a convoy of seven vehicles but had become detached and, by all accounts, a little deranged over the past two days. His other problem is that it is forbidden to cross this stretch of desert alone, so he'll probably get stuck in Ain Guezzam police station tomorrow. Half an hour after turning round we saw three motorbikes coming towards us. We flagged them down to tell them that it was the wrong piste. In the soft sand one of the Italians fell off as he slowed. They told me that they must ride at over 50 mph to stay on the bikes in the soft sand. They also decided to turn around and they soon vanished in a cloud of dust. Before long we saw the French cars again. They told us they had found the proper piste and had come back to tell us where it was. Soon enough we were back on the comforting corrugations. The piste deteriorated into a confusion of rocky tracks with deep soft sand in the hollows.

Later we came across a motorbike and one of the Italians was sitting under it with his tent draped over it for shade. The sun was now white hot and you could almost hear the wavering squeal of violins if you looked up towards it. The front hub of the bike was smashed, he didn't have a spare. He had missed a gear change in the soft sand, lost control and hit a rock. His friends had gone on, promising to send a truck back from Ain Guezzam, a hundred kilometres further on (although we never heard anything more of them).

So, sooner than expected, and fulfilling the wishes in my last letter, I was able to offer hospitality to someone in need, thus feeling more entitled to the hospitality *we* have so far received. We tied the bike to the side of the truck, loaded his luggage and headed for Assamakka. He was lucky indeed – the piste being very wide with many parallel tracks running between the rocky hills – that we had chosen to take the same one that he had done.

Border formalities have taken most of the day but it has all gone smoothly enough. We are now on the well-marked piste to Arlit. We have camped by some small sand dunes in an endless plain. After we stopped I just had to go for a run. Once over the shallow dune I threw off my shorts and ran naked over this naked world. I ran and ran until I could no longer see or hear the group, or in fact anything apart from the wispy clouds, the horizon and sunset. What a feeling; surely *this* is freedom! The silence whistled through my head and I stood dead centre in a still calm sea; dry and lifeless; and yet somehow it seemed the whole world was there, and I felt as though I'd been here forever.

Arlit, the first town in Niger, is, after five weeks' travelling, the first taste of Africa for the group. It also felt like a kind of 'welcome home' for me. I'd forgotten how much I love Africa. It's the smiles, the continual greetings and always the sound of laughter, even in this dusty, dirty, uranium mining desert town. It's the men, asking where you are from and where you are going, reaching out to shake your hand. It's the women with their sing-song laughing gossip, dressed in colourful, printed dresses and head-scarves, and it's the children, albeit demanding; nevertheless always cheerful and open.

We spent several hours here whilst the police stamped our passports and I bought insurance for the truck. I found that during my 'holiday' in Europe I'd slipped back to a degree, into the European time scale and found myself getting just a little frustrated at the 'slowly, slowly' attitude here. It's a question of adjustment, that's all.

Now that this is my third journey through Africa, I feel more qualified than before to make comparisons and contrasts with the 'Western' world. It seems that there are a good many people in Europe and the USA who feel that, for all the advantages of technological advancement, something intangible has been sacrificed. Perhaps it's necessary; Africa herself is sacrificing the same thing right now, but I'd like to try to identify this in these letters. I think it is not something that can be learned but something we've learned to forget, and I, like most other 'Westerners' have indeed forgotten it in most aspects of my life.

It's my birthday today and I've promised to cook dinner. I went shopping in the vegetable market in Arlit. It was fairly limited; onions, tomatoes, carrots, and a kind of sweet potato and some bananas, but for less than £10 I reckoned I had got enough to feed twenty-two. The food so far on the trip has been okay but only okay. There has been far too much reliance on the tinned and dehydrated stores we carry and these have been supplemented rather unimaginatively with a few vegetables bought locally. People have to learn to turn their existing ideas about cooking on their heads and instead of deciding what to make and then getting wound up when they can't find it, must see what is available, then decide what it can be made into. Once this has been recognised, the quality of the meals improves dramatically. I used to find it very difficult myself. I remember when I was hop-picking in Kent, living with fifteen people and I had to take my turn at cooking. I dreaded it.

Everyone else seemed to just 'chuck it all in' and turn out delicious meals but I was afraid to do that, I wanted a recipe book to do it for me. Since then, with much trial and error, I've learned something of what works and what doesn't. I've never stopped experimenting and have made it a rule never to cook the same thing twice.

Well, for my birthday, from the group, I got a card made from an 'Angel Whirl' packet (it's a bit of a joke as we have so much and I don't like it!) and inside were passport photos of everyone, which was a good idea. As a present I got a bucketful of bottles of beer which, of course, were shared out for the party. I proposed we have a 'dishco' in which the drying up of the plates, etc., is done by waving them about whilst dancing. Out came Michael Jackson and soon most people were hopping and bopping in the sand.

Our Italian motorcycle friend is having more than his fair share of adventure. Whilst putting down his tent next morning he was stung on the finger by a scorpion. He was a bit worried but it wasn't serious and only caused him pain for a couple of days.

Agadez; hot and outwardly very friendly but they've seen too many tourists here and it is hard to avoid being ripped off. What *we* have and they don't is far more tangible than the things they have and we don't, and, as a result, most Africans are aspiring materialists.

The children always ask for gifts. The shopkeepers inflate their prices and agreed prices tend to go up unexpectedly. I've got sick and tired of the inevitable arguments about the bill we've had every time we've eaten out. Now the group has learned the lesson that all such groups learn sooner or later; to look after their bags. During the night of the fourteenth of

March thieves sneaked into the camp and stole away with two bags containing expensive cameras and the like. Luckily for my passengers and for me, they had not kept their passports there.

The desert gives way to sparse vegetation in fits and starts as though it were running out of petrol. This is not to say that it doesn't have definite boundary; it does. It ended as abruptly as it had started in the Atlas mountains but this front is the scene of battle and massacre. A ten kilometre front line belt of death and destruction. The bleached bones of trees lie twisted where they writhed and gasped their last as they are smothered in the advancing desert oven.

And then there are squat mud or grass houses and villages, cattle and stretching landscapes of dry maize. These people may yet be vanquished, but weary as they are of the struggle, they haven't given up. There are several small tree nurseries and some tree planting programmes are being carried out by the people. There is room for much more, but it is a start. They always ask for presents, the women holding snotty, fly covered babies, eagerly accept dry bread, tin cans and bottles.

In Agadez we'd actually watched television; Niger TV 'Voice of the Sahel', an interesting programme covering a traditional music festival followed by a contemporary Nigerienne fashion show. Perhaps the most interesting aspect, however, was that each TV was placed outside and had a crowd of fifty to a hundred people standing and sitting around it. I thought about the cars and pick-up trucks here, always crammed with people, four across the front seat, ten in a lorry cab, thirty in a pick-up truck. Refreshing to see these unaffordable items, so taken for granted at home, bringing people together, when between them they are perhaps the main elements for driving people apart in the developed world. It is like water, even in this arid country – give the people an engine-driven water-pump or pipe the water to their houses and you would make their lives a little easier perhaps, but at the same time you'd destroy the main focus of their community and, in time, the community itself. In just a few decades in Britain we have seen this important aspect of life all but disappear. Certainly it was not all roses before that, as it is not here now, and it has certainly given us the time to develop further, but are we really using this time to its full advantage – chasing our tails in our cars, blotting out our creativity with our televisions and, above all, ceasing to relate to other people with a sense of common purpose?

Niamey, capital of Niger. I hadn't been here before but it was exactly as I had imagined. We've passed through about twenty police checks in two days since Agadez. In major towns we must all get our passports stamped at the Police Stations. Now, here in the capital, they also require a photograph and give us two stamps.

The mornings are like beautiful, clear summer days at home but by midday the heat is thick and hard to breathe. The salty sweat runs into my eyes as I write. In the afternoons the temperature is approaching 120° F and everything shuts down until 4.00pm. To break with English tradition, I don't venture out with the mad dogs.

I don't enjoy these big African towns very much. My thinking gets muggy in the heat. People walk in the road and I have to drive very slowly and be alert to avoid the inevitable unexpected. The traffic lights don't work and the road junctions are unclear. My indicators have stopped working. We find the camp site and as I sit down to lunch the man from the camp site wants to see my passport and the passenger list. He tells me that the police station is closed until 4.00pm. I have a cold shower – great, but only fifteen minutes later I am running with sweat again. At 4.00pm we take the truck into town and find the police station. I take in all the passports and photographs and get sent around three offices. The policeman wants to see everyone. I tell everyone to put on long trousers or skirts and bring pens. This takes almost twenty minutes, by which time the policeman is getting very impatient. We all complete the forms we are given and it seems that, for each question on the form, I am asked the answer ten times, and that's after I'd already gone through it for everyone. It's getting hard to keep my replies helpful and matter-of-fact.

I'd borrowed Algerian money off everyone in Algeria to help them spend the money they have to change, so all day people have been asking me when they can be repaid in CFAs. I'd so far only been able to change cash, as it's not possible to change travellers' cheques outside Niamey. I asked the policeman when the bank closes.

"Six o'clock," he said.

It was now 5.00pm and by the time we got our passports back, it was 5.35pm. The bank closed at 5.00pm. I have only 5,000 CFA notes (about £10) but they might as well be roubles because nobody ever has any change. Now this means that I have to come back to the Bank in the morning (Wednesday), then go to the Benin Embassy and apply for visas in twenty-four hours or else we'll be here till Monday. Mats, the Swede, who had his camera stolen in Agadez, asks me if it will be a problem if he flies to Togo so that he can buy a new one. Someone else asks why we can't move the truck nearer the market, even though half the people have already gone and we have arranged to meet here at 6.30pm.

Around the truck are twenty or thirty boys and men who wrangle with each other to push their wares at me.

"Coca Cola?"

"Non, merci."

"Jewellery?"

"Non, merci."

"Monsieur, monsieur, donnez moi un cadeau." (give me a gift).

"No cadeau."

"Monsieur, cigarettes?"

"Je ne fume pas."

"Coca cola?"

"Leather boxes?"

"Straw hats?"

"Peanuts?"

It is sometimes necessary to use the international phrase coined by Billy Connolly which I shall not repeat here; suffice to say that it works very well!

I escaped and walked alone with almost no money and absolutely no hassle to the new market. It's a superb complex, modern, clean, but in the best African tradition. I was impressed. It was spoilt a little, though, by a large open sewer that ran beside it and the many nauseating smells often caught me with empty lungs! It is no easy task to describe such towns as this to people who have not been out of Europe. The unmetalled street are thickly lined with people sitting or squatting, talking, cooking in woks over small charcoal stoves or cooking meat on open fires. Some are making bedsteads or selling heaps of assorted junk and scrap. Small boys selling cigarettes from trays on their heads. Children leading blind parents around by the hand asking for charity. People sleeping and people washing clothes. Step over the festering puddles, hold your breath past the sewer vents and watch out for the mopeds and the taxis. It probably sounds awful but it does have a sort of anarchic appeal and they are not always dirty as this.

Anyway I will close this now and get it posted. All the best to everyone.

Love,
Graham.

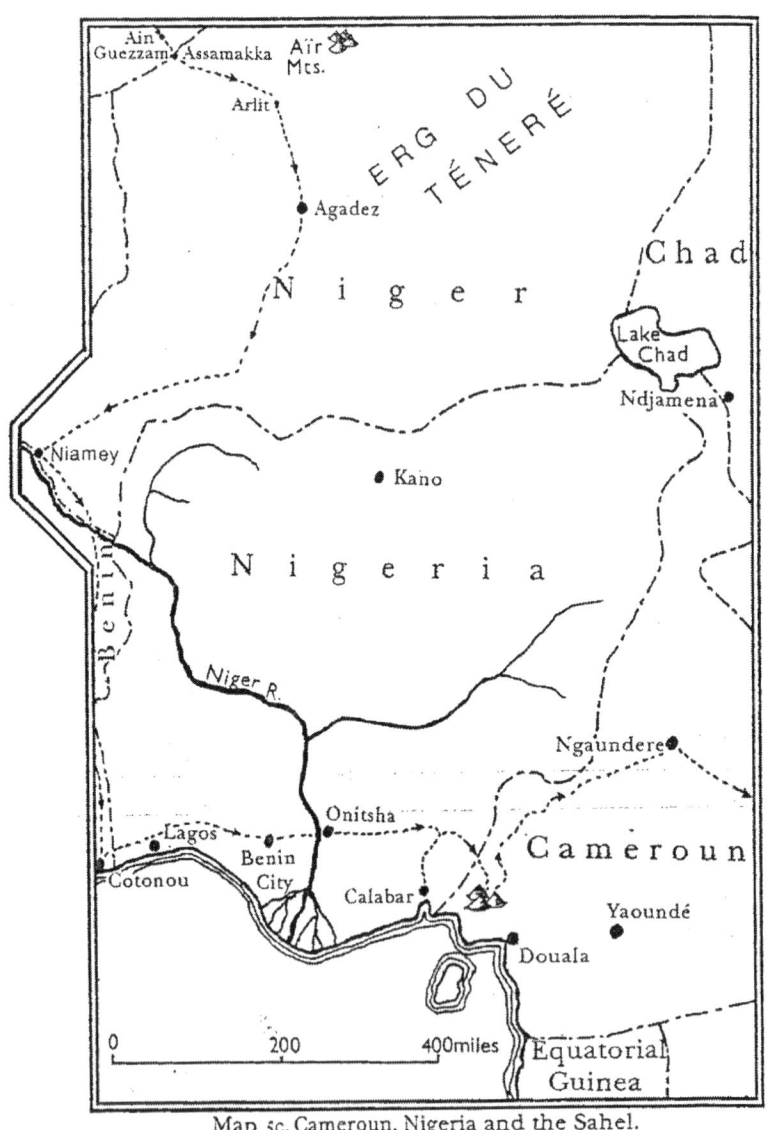

Map 5c. Cameroun, Nigeria and the Sahel.

Cotonou, Benin.
29th March, 1987

Dear All

I'm now in Benin which used to be called Dahomey. It's a small country between Togo and Nigeria. We wouldn't normally have come here but the Nigerian Embassy in Niamey is taking up to six weeks to issue visas. The one here in Cotonou isn't easy but once they decide whether or not to give visas they'll do it in twenty-four hours.

It's not very long since the military coup here and the police and army are much in evidence and not always very friendly. There's also a law here against camping. We had to risk it one night as there was nowhere else but wouldn't want to have been caught. The following night we found some cheap basic accommodation in a village; three bare rooms. We parked there and cooked in the village itself amongst the huts and the people. That evening Sam and I went down to the local 'pub', a thatched, round shelter lit with paraffin lamps. Here we met an American Peace Corps Volunteer. She'd been living in this village for six months and was involved in a project installing hand-operated water pumps in the villages of this area. They have a serious problem here with a water-borne parasite known as 'Guinea-worm'. These can grow inside you up to a metre in length and occasionally pop out through the skin. It's incurable, even using western medicine and in some villages 50% suffer from it. The easiest way of countering it is to provide clean water, which is the aim of the project, by drilling new bore holes. She also said that she occasionally helped with vaccination and was horrified to find they've been using the same syringe and needle on the whole district for a couple of years. It's apparently now so blunt that it's hard to push in. The Government here is still at the stage of East African countries a couple of years ago in denying they have an AIDS problem. There is also no shortage of 'bar' girls or prostitutes here. Prostitution in Africa isn't really the same as that in Europe. Very often it's just any girl who sees a chance, not of making a lot of money, but of being treated for the evening. A few drinks, perhaps a meal, or just some attention. Of course, there are the more professional ladies, and white men are always favourites as they are seen, usually rightly, as having the most money.

Back at our three bare rooms we have dinner and retire early. Those wanting to use the toilet had to put up with sharing it with the biggest cockroaches I've ever seen (and I thought I'd *seen* the biggest!). Down the narrow passageway, taking care not to brush against the walls lest one of these four-inch (six-inch with the feelers!) creatures should hitch a lift. Then into the tiny cubicle with a hole in the floor. The dark red wallpaper scuttled and scratched away in the torchlight and, from the small holes, long feelers could be seen checking out this new intrusion. Keep scanning that light to keep them hiding, or they'll be SKRIKKETING up your legs!

Undeniably, good standards of hygiene and health care are something that the developed world has to its advantage. That is not to say that Africans are dirty; individually they are very clean, but all too often, be it through lack of planning, responsibility, or realisation, such things as open sewers, latrines next to wells and the like will inevitably take their roll on the health of the people. Conversely, hygiene can be taken too far as in the case of the Japanese I met in Marrakech. They walked into the hotel restaurant wearing surgeons' masks. I thought it was some sort of gimmick or joke but no... They asked the manageress to close the windows and doors and, when their meal arrived, the simultaneously lowered their masks to eat. Once they finished, up went the masks again – took a deep breath and out they went! They were part of a large Japanese coach tour, all dressed the same and I was surprised to learn that it's not uncommon for Japanese in Tokyo to wear such masks for protection against germs.

Now, you may think we're having a pretty rough time but, at this moment, due to Benin's 'No Camping' law, I'm lounging beside the swimming pool of a very nice hotel, beneath the coconut palms. We've been here three days now and each day I've visited immigration and the Nigerian Embassy at least twice trying first to get Benin visa extensions and then trying to persuade the Nigerians to let us into Nigeria. It's hot, sticky work, especially wearing long trousers, arguing prices with taxi-drivers, waiting to see officials, being sent elsewhere.

I grabbed a break today and sat outside a cafe. I'd only been there a minute when a crippled man came past with a blind man on each arm. The three of them stopped and began to sing. Two of them sang a repetitive, rhythmic bass and a third sang a harmony over the top; he was blind with a deformed mouth but, as he sang, an unmistakable joy came over his grotesque face that flooded over to me. I paid these wretched men for the food they must eat and not out of the terrible pity that most other beggars rely on. They did not thank me for the money but, when they'd finished singing, mumbled a prayer and thanked Allah; for it had, indeed, been Allah that had provided it.

The music here is real, inspired and inspiring - not the distraction it has largely become back in 'civilisation'. Bury your head in your Sony Walkman to hide from this cruel world and everything's okay. Of course, not all recorded Western music is dreary commercialism and noisy distraction. It has had several injections of life, inspiration and spontaneity itself over the years. Interesting, though, to ponder that many of the recent such injections should be provided by people of African descent; Jazz, Rock and Roll, Blues, Funk, Soul, Reggae.

A boy of about eleven came up to me with a single stringed instrument he'd made from pieces of wood, wire and a large tin can. I've seen many similar instruments in Africa - crude home-made guitars with wrongly spaced frets and any old wire for strings. Also, strange bow-like instruments made from gourds, sticks and wire, technically hopelessly inaccurate and completely imprecise, but they soon get everyone tapping their feet, singing along or watching silently in awe as the performer becomes the performance.

As I walked past the truck one day, one of the elastic straps was stretched under a hook. I twanged it aimlessly and discovered that on either side of the hook the note was different but in harmony and I found myself twanging a rhythm that, for a moment, sounded quite good. I got to thinking that musical spontaneity seems to flow from apparent freedom. You can buy a synthesiser in civilisation and it will make any sound you want, re-create any beat you choose, but it's no more likely to help you play 'real' music than that single stringed tin can. Probably less, in fact, because it offers so many possibilities that you wouldn't know where to start. I wondered if perhaps this couldn't apply to other contrasts between our ways of life. The simple life here, the lack of complexity or confusion, seems to leave room for the wonderful, almost child-like sense of humour, fun and cheerfulness, even in the face of often severe hardship and suffering.

In our world we've opened out the possibilities to such an extent that most people don't know where to begin. Their spontaneity is lost and they're so distracted by all the knobs, switches and keys of the synthesiser that they realise they don't know what they were doing here in the first place. Africans probably don't know either but, in both cases, the aim is surely to enjoy playing the music that others can enjoy listening to it. Africans don't seem to think about it, they just do it.

Well, after my fourth interview with the Nigerian Ambassador in three days, I've eventually got our visas. I spent over four hours there this morning – waiting – waiting, but, anyway. Now we can leave tomorrow so, until the next letter...

Hope everything's all right with you all.

Love,
Graham.

Near Jakiri, North West Cameroun
5 April, 1987

Dear All

We've come to the mountains here in Cameroun for a day or two of relaxation and walking. We're actually a little ahead of our schedule which makes a nice change.

We got through Nigeria without serious event which was a relief after the horror stories I'd heard about the south of the country. People in Niger and Benin became concerned when we told them that we were next going to Nigeria.

"There are many thieves there."

"Niger okay, Benin no problem but Nigeria is a bad place."

"Don't cross the Nigerian border at night or they'll shoot you and steal your money."

Of course, most of these people have probably never been there and my own experience of the north of Nigeria was that of genuine friendliness and a relaxed atmosphere. The south is far more populated and although most people are very friendly we all left with a bad taste in our memories and agreed that Nigeria is, in many ways, 'Europe gone crazy'. The government's fight against decadence and social disintegration is all but lost. It's hard to believe that it could ever be what it once aspired to be. The rot is to the core.

The border from Benin was straightforward enough, despite having to give the Nigerian customs officer fifteen dollars. Now we were faced with road checks, sometimes every 5kms. The police, military or gendarmes, depending on whose road check it is, don't carry pistols but wield machine guns and high velocity automatic rifles. Quite often they're not all in uniform which can be more than a little disconcerting though we didn't have any problems with them. They're usually after money but they didn't do any more than ask. I kept a count of roadblocks; in two days we'd been stopped at fifty-one. I saw in a newspaper an article by a top Chief of Police who condemned the police for setting up illegal roadblocks and intimidating people. He said they'd now become masters of the community rather than servants to it.

The roads are busy here, like England, except that the drivers don't seem to associate driving fast and recklessly with the countless mangled wrecks that they pass every quarter of a mile or so, often still partly on the road. At about 4.30pm near Lagos we drove into a small town. The traffic clogged to a stop. As far as we could see the traffic was stopped. Many drivers, especially the minibus and taxi drivers, tried to by-pass the jam by driving down the wrong side of the road. When they eventually got stuck all the traffic at our end was facing the same way, five cars across on a normal road. This, of course, meant that, despite any obstruction causing the hold-up, no-one would be able to come towards us anyway. We figured that it was likely to be the same story at the other end. Most drivers showed incredible patience, as though they sat through this every night.

I walked ahead to see what was the cause. I walked for half an hour and still all I could see were cars and trucks all over the place, now with their engines turned off. At length I realised that all the vehicles were facing the other way, so I thought I could safely assume that I'd passed the halfway point. There had been no dreadful accident, no broken-down truck, nothing. Simply inconsiderate driving that had caused the whole thing. It's got to be the most chaotic traffic jam I've seen in all my life and it took us until well after dark to get out of there. I was glad to find a roadside restaurant that had cheap rooms and a walled car park. They also had a TV and tonight on the news they featured the much publicised execution of a man who, last year, had robbed various places and shot fifteen policemen. He was to be publicly executed along with three other lesser criminals by the usual method of five or six volleys from a firing squad, starting at the ankles and pausing in between each shot. I couldn't bring myself to watch it on the news but the double-page blow-by-blow account in the next day's paper was more than enough. I've kept the paper but wouldn't recommend anyone to read it. I remember it was Sir Robert Peel, the Prime Minister who introduced the police force to Britain in the nineteenth Century, who said that the most important factor in the reduction of crime was not, as had previously been supposed, the severity of the punishment, but the certainty of being caught.

There are many policemen in Nigeria, even too many, but such is the level of corruption and crimes such as armed robbery that the capture is by no means certain. Of course, no armed robber goes out with the intention of getting caught, just as car drivers don't overtake on blind bends with the intention of meeting a truck coming the other way. The result, however, is pretty much the same for both. Even if they were executed cleanly, all it does is satisfy the morbid curiosity of the thousands of spectators in the stadium and millions of newspaper readers and TV viewers. I suppose it saves on prison bills but it also creates a public acceptance of a high level of violence in the society. It also means that victims of armed robbery are much more likely to be killed to prevent them identifying their assailant; after all, the punishment is the same. This environment breeds armed robber mentality.

It also breeds religious fervour. The roads here are lined with churches, missions, bible schools and meeting halls of every branch of Christianity you've never heard of. In the north it's the same except it's Moslem. Most of the trucks are painted with 'circus' type slogans across the cabs or on the back, such as:-

"Praise the Lord."

"Blessed."

"God's Destiny Transport Ltd."

"God's time is the only time."

Often they have verses from the Bible written complete on the back. There are similar bill-boards on the roadside sponsored by various Churches. (With 'Exodus Expeditions' written on our cab we're often mistaken for a religious tour group associated with the Book of Exodus.)

It seems as though all these Churches are competing for a slice of the cake around here. There are, no doubt, many 'lost' souls but perhaps more to the point there was, until only a few years ago, a lot of money here that came with the oil boom.

Evidence of the collapse of the oil boom is everywhere; half built houses and churches are strewn across the country, never to be completed. The towns that set out to become modern, European-style towns have degenerated into dirty, rubbish-filled, crime-ridden, hell-holes. The sad fact is that in Nigeria, African inspirations to Westernisation thought they had found the means to its realisation. No doubt Western businesses sold the idea pretty hard as well. Cars, concrete, roads, TVs, industry, intensive agriculture, intensive housing. But it fed only the greed and the division of an already divided nation and now it all seems to have gone terribly wrong.

We saw a dead child lying in the road like a dog. Nobody stopped and nor did we, for to risk being blamed would be to risk being lynched.

One night we camped just outside a village. The villagers came to chat with us and were friendly, but just after dinner a minibus-load of policemen with automatic rifles drew up and encircled us, demanding to know what we were up to. They tore film out of two cameras because they suspected we'd taken photos and then told us to move. They led us to a church in the next town and a policeman with a Kalashnikov rode in my cab. By the church was some flat grass and was okay. While the group re-erected the tents, Sam and I had to go and meet the local police chief. As expected, he tried to find fault with our documentation so as to extract bribes but it was all in order. We were then told to see the immigration officer who was in the bar although turned out to be a decent guy. The priest had been ordered to put us up and was a bit shy to start with. In the morning, however, he came down to organise an impromptu service for our departure.

Nigerian border exit formalities took an incredible six hours despite there being about fifteen staff on duty and virtually no-one else crossing. When we left to drive across the bridge to the Cameroun entry point it was dark and we were in the middle of a torrential downpour. The Cameroun border officials were very helpful and told us that there was another overland truck camped just outside town. They said that, if we left our passports, we could go and spend the night with them and return the following morning. It was a group from Guerba Expeditions. All their tents had fallen down in the rain. We had dinner, then all went across the road to a small open-air bar where there was African disco music playing. We had a good party; for us a celebration at leaving Nigeria, for them a sad farewell to Cameroun.

It's good to meet other groups and gratifying to see that my group is so well-organised. Groups always tend to come away from meetings with other groups criticising the other's systems of work allocation, etc. It seems, though, that people can adapt and learn to work within any system, however ill-conceived it may be. It has been my personal mission to design a system that will go furthest towards eliminating unnecessary tensions within the group. The system I have evolved is based on one I read about in a self-contained village community in France. In this, each person performs each of the many different skills and tasks for one month and then moves on to the next. Each person, therefore, has first-hand experience of every job and, although they may not be good at them all, it does provide an excellent opportunity to broaden individual skills. The aspect of the system that appeals to me most is that the job of chief is also rotated and this includes the responsibility for looking after the manure!

In the latest manifestation of my system, the cooking is done in pairs and each person cooks once every six days. The pairs are never the same to encourage continual mixing of the people and to prevent cliques. The same applies to washing up. Chopping wood and lighting the fires are done by a different person each day. Many people find this job hard to start with and often complain that they 'just can't light fires'. By the end of the trip there's no-one who can't! It is my hope that people will leave these trips feeling more able to tackle such jobs. Men who've never cooked before often find that they *enjoy* cooking for twenty-two. I've also included 'vehicle maintenance' on this trip's rota. Everyone must, in turn adjust the brakes, check the various oil levels and check the tightness of the nuts and bolts. I've found everyone to be eager to get involved in this and I'm sure they'll get more out of the trip if they feel that *they* got this truck through Africa and didn't just sit there and be dragged through. I let everyone have fifteen minutes each at the wheel in the desert; they all enjoyed that, even though I have two people who'd never driven anything before. They can now go home and say they actually drove the truck (they don't have to say for how long).

Every trip sees new changes to the work rota. People often suggest additions or subtractions; sometimes they're worth including in the next, sometimes they're not practicable, but we always discuss it and so it is the various groups that change the system, not just me.

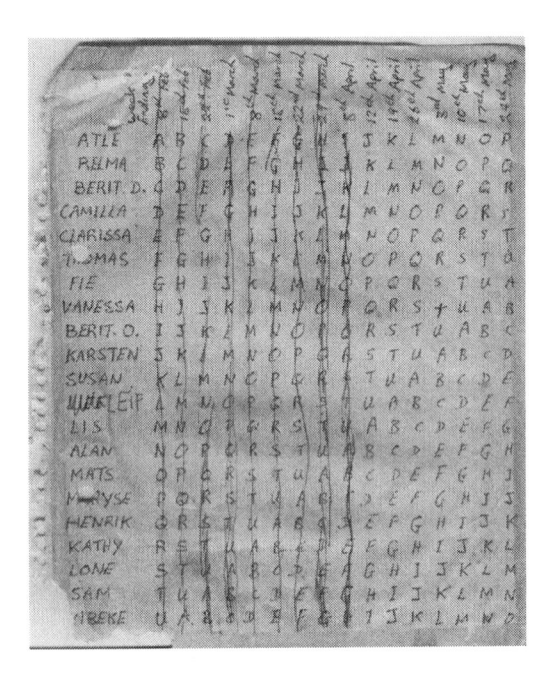

The key for the rota on the next page

	Monday	Tuesday	Wednesday	Thursday	Friday	Saturday	Makaravedag
A	\multicolumn{7}{c	}{WATER}
B	shopping cooking	Security	Security		Security		Fire
C	wash-up + put away	shopping cooking		Security		Security	
D		wash-up + put away	shopping cooking		Security		Security
E	Fire		wash-up + put away	shopping cooking		Security	
F	\multicolumn{7}{c	}{STORES, CLEANING, RUBBISH + LATRINES}
G		Fire		wash-up + put away	shopping cooking		Security
H	Security		Fire		wash-up + put away	shopping cooking	
I		Security		Fire		wash-up + put away	shopping cooking
J	Security		Security		Fire		wash-up + put away
K	\multicolumn{7}{c	}{MAINTENANCE}
L	Security	Security		Security		Fire	
M	Security		Security		Tents		wash-up + put away
N		Security		Tents		wash-up + put away	shopping cooking
O			Tents	Security		wash-up + put away	shopping cooking
P	\multicolumn{7}{c	}{STORES, CLEANING, RUBBISH + LATRINES}
Q		Tents		wash-up + put away	shopping cooking		Security
R	Tents		wash-up + put away	shopping cooking		Security	
S		wash-up + put away	shopping cooking		Security		Security
T	wash-up + put away	shopping cooking		Security		Security	Tents
U	shopping cooking		Security		Security	Tents	

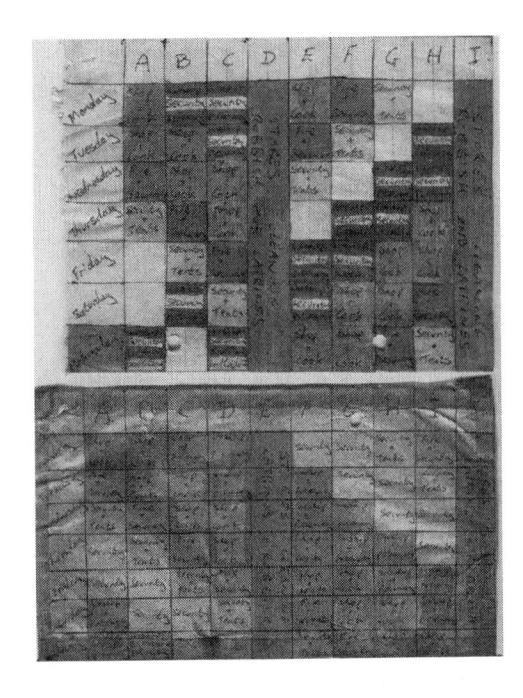

My rotas had to be re-drawn for different group sizes

Another of our drivers had told me that in the very north-western corner of Cameroun we'd find the friendliest people in Africa. This has certainly been verified by our group. The area is also English-speaking which obviously greatly increases our communication with local people.

"Hey, White Man!" you'll hear in the market.

"Yes?" you may answer guardedly.

"How are you?" will come the smiling reply.

We took the road from Mamfe to Bamenda which passes through some of the most spectacular rainforest I've seen. Steep hills and deep valleys jungled with hanging green and two-hundred foot columns. Screeching, chirping and chattering – no sign of man. With our increase in altitude the climate is once again comfortable and should stay more or less this way for the rest of the trip. Like a pleasant summer day in England - it even rains sometimes!

One of the women in the group has developed a large boil on the back of her neck. It's very painful and we've tried all sorts to no avail. She was rather worried about it so I agreed to find a doctor in Bamenda. Bamenda is quite a big town and, by the time we'd found that the doctor wasn't on duty until 8.00am, it was 6.00pm. I asked a man, who claimed to be a policeman, where we could stay and he suggested we camp at the Baptist Mission. He also said that they had a 'hospital' there.

We soon found it; a large complex of low buildings amongst green lawns and trees. We were immediately met by 'Pat', a kindly American missionary who'd been here since 1963. She said that we were welcome to camp and showed us the toilets and showers and where to pitch our tents. She looked at the boil and said that, although their clinic hadn't got a qualified doctor, the nurse was quite used to such complaints which are common around here. He also came on duty at 8.00am but she advised us that somebody should start queuing at 5.00am as it's first come first served.

At 4.45am there were already ten people waiting. By 8.00am there were more than three hundred and fifty!

The waiting hall was a mass of rich colours and screaming babies. As each in turn went into the surgery, everyone stood up and moved one seat. It was very well ordered. The nurse on duty was good and Mats, our Swedish student doctor, was very impressed by his swift diagnosis with the minimum of equipment and formal training. By the look of the waiting room, though, one day's work would be as good as a year in College! Other people waiting said they preferred to come here rather than the hospital as the people seemed to care more and also supplied the medicines direct rather than sending you off on a wild goose chase around the pharmacies for drugs that weren't available.

Apart from running the clinic, the mission also had a dentist's surgery once a week and provided training for local people in a variety of skills from teaching to plumbing and motor vehicle repairs. This goes right against the traditional image of the missionary as a well-meaning but misguided bible-basher, intent on turning all these 'savages' into good God-fearing Christians. As long as they're providing such constructive and much-needed services they have my wholehearted support.

Originally it was the early explorers such as Mungo Park and David Livingstone who encouraged the influx of missionaries to Africa. They'd found the Africans to be often dishonest and impoverished through, as they saw it, their 'lack of God'. It's interesting to note that Tanzania has just recently sent its first missionary to West Germany.

The walk today has done everyone a power of good. It's been a bit rushed this last week so what better than to come to the mountains on this beautiful, hazy summer's day. The group soon divided on the walk which was no bad thing as it meant we were better accepted in people's houses. One woman told us she'd seen one white man and that was three years ago!

I found some peace whilst walking; even though I was in a crowd, I was alone, but it only gave me an appetite for more solitude. At times like this I feel like vanishing into the forest to live like a wild man.

We were given cola-nuts, avocados, guided tours of huts, peanuts and then, in the morning before we left, one woman walked five miles to give us two eggs and a live chicken.

So now we're in Bangui, capital of the Central African Republic. I've had a lot to sort out here; Zaire visas, insurance, letter writing, persuading the bank that I've had £3,000 sent (again, today's task – day three), and seeing two people off to hospital. That boil I mentioned turned out to be an enormous carbuncle and didn't appear to be getting any better. Also our French lady has developed one on her leg, apart from badly gashing her foot in a river and getting a stone stuck in the wound. I did warn them that hospitals here are not what you'd expect to find at home – but they insisted.

At 8.00am they arrived at the large hospital and began waiting. They managed to get seen by 10.00am which was quite a feat considering the crowd of other people waiting. The doctor decided to operate in both cases. Martine asked for a glass of water as she was so thirsty so the surgeon led her along corridors, downstairs, through doors, past the families of relatives who've moved in from the countryside to be near their sick ones. These relatives were washing clothes, cooking over open fires, sleeping in the corridors or in make-shift shanty towns in the grounds. Hundreds of people, children and babies and dogs running around in the hospital. He led her at last to a dark corridor lined with bins full of old bandages, bloody sheets and bits of flesh – old and stinking – into his small room where he had a fridge. He produced a bottle, black around the rim, filled with cloudy water. He apologised for it not being fresh but Martine was too thirsty to care and drank it anyway.

Back outside the operating theatre the doctors were arguing as to whether to give her a local or general anaesthetic. They'd already decided that Freja, our other patient, should have a general. As each patient was finished, they were trundled to one side and the next trundled into place. Martine's turn came and they strapped her down with leather straps. Freja and Martine had had to buy various medicines, bandages, needles, etc., though Martine was certain they'd used old needles anyway. They gave her a general anaesthetic and she wimpered and struggled to sleep. The surgeon, in old plastic wellies, ordinary clothes, plastic apron and yellowed, cracked plastic gloves, started work while no doubt tapping his feet to the blaring radio or talking to the multitudes of people who were milling around or just coming in for a look.

Despite the horror of this scene, the patients were very impressed by the friendliness and care of the doctors and said they'd rarely seen such in Europe. The doctors even refused payment despite there being no other way for their being paid – and they offered to come to the campsite free of charge the next day to change the dressings.

Hopefully, all is now well – and I've just heard from another driver that my money has arrived, so we leave for Zaire tomorrow.

All the best to you all,

Love, Graham.

Map 6c. The Zaire river basin.

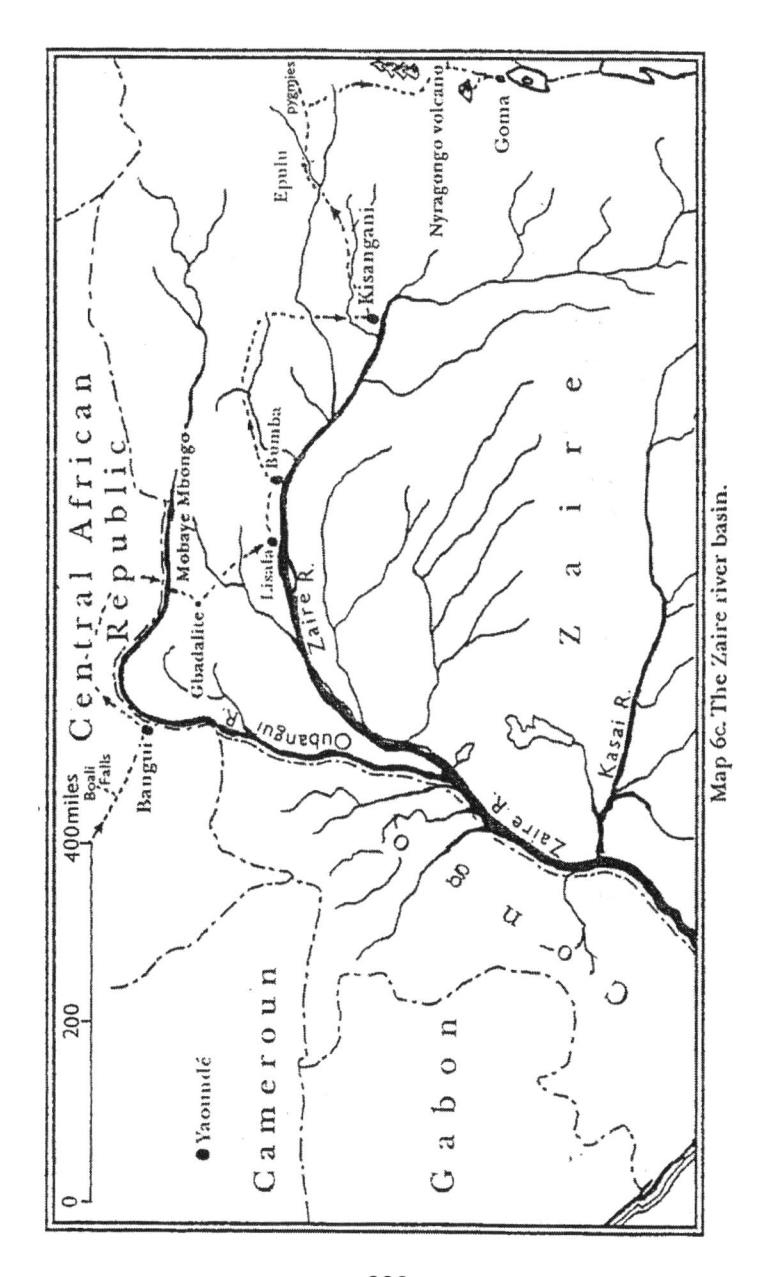

40km south of Businga, Zaire
19th April 1987

Dear All

We managed to get out of Bangui without getting ripped off which is little short of a miracle considering the number of thefts each day from travellers. We have a twenty-four hour watch as does everyone camping there and still people try and jump over the fence. The previous week there was a theft every night despite the all-night watch. We'd met an Italian man and a French woman travelling in a Land Rover. I saw it parked unattended – unwise! Ten minutes later there were two guys inside helping themselves to bags and clothes. I walked towards it purposefully though not quite sure what I was going to do. Luckily they saw me and nonchalantly walked away, apparently empty-handed. I stayed with it until the owners returned. They had lost one bag but nothing too valuable. An Englishman on the camp-site had his Land Rover broken into whilst he was sleeping in it and lost a bag. The next day he parked outside a cafe and sat at one of the roadside tables ten feet away. He'd looked away for just a few seconds but enough time for the window to be forced and all his clothes stolen. Another traveller was sitting in his vehicle guarding it whilst, unbeknown to him, two men were on the roof unlocking his jerry-cans! They were spotted by another traveller who chased them away. I could go on, in fact I'm sure I could write a book on thefts in Africa and at least 50% of it would be set in Bangui!

Good to be back in the country with country people. They're so much more friendly in eastern Central African Republic, though that's not to say they're unfriendly elsewhere, even in Bangui.

We found a place to camp near a village and had the usual crowd of spectators, mainly children. Ants were swarming and they clouded around the lights dying into our dinner. Everyone was flapping and swatting.

"It will rain tonight" announced a young man of about twenty.

I wasn't so sure but most people decided to straighten out their fly-sheets and batten down the hatches anyway. 'Civilised' people are very eager to believe that simple people such as these have got these things sussed out. It's unfortunate that it prevents them ever trying to suss it out for themselves. We are, after all, living outside too.

"How come the locals don't get bothered by these bugs" complained Martine. But I pointed out that they too were being driven crazy by them and some of the children were terrified of a particularly large bug that I knew to be harmless and, indeed, edible. I was reminded of a meeting with a traveller in Algeria who was interested in astronomy. He thought to spend a night with nomads in the desert so that he might glean some useful information, Arabs being the inventors of astronomy. The moonless night sky blazed shimmering as he sat beside the small fire sipping sugary tea with the desert herdsmen. At a suitable lull, he picked out the piercing North Star and asked:

"What would you call that star in your language?" as an introduction to the ensuing astronomical discussion.

"Ur... I dunno really," came the shattering reply. "Hey Mustafa!"

"Yeah."

"'Ere, what do we call that star?"

"Which one?"

"The bright one over there."

"I dunno, it's just a star, innit?"

So much for their profound knowledge of the cosmos, for their legacy of navigational innovations that we would now be lost without!

You may be sorry to hear that I've given up recording music with my tape-recorder. Firstly, because it gets through batteries faster than I can buy them, secondly, because I rarely have it with me when music unexpectedly happens and thirdly because I played back some of the things I'd taped. What had sounded beautiful at the time now sounds like so much jingle-jangle, likely only to convey a picturesque and patronising view of these 'primitives' to people back home. The real content of the music remains unrecorded and unrecordable. It is music created and performed wholly in the 'here and now' and so can never be transported to the 'there and then'.

And indeed, here we are, here and now, in Zaire where there *is* only today. Nothing here looks new except for the affluent 'village' of Gbadalite and nothing looks old, except for the decaying colonial buildings of Kisangani. For most people here there is little progress towards 'development' and little evidence of their history because it is all happening now. From the well-dressed bank managers to the Neanderthal existence of the pygmies, today is the only day. It is to be used and enjoyed but not to get wound up about. If you don't kill a gazelle today there'll be no food tonight and maybe better luck tomorrow. If the paperwork isn't finished, there's always more time and anyway, chatting with your friends is just as important a pastime. I don't mean to be cynical, this is the attitude that will drive any European crazy who tries to resist it. My trip now runs on Zairian fundamentals and things only go wrong when I forget that and try to make things happen myself.

I saw six men loading a lorry with beer. Standing in a line, glossy, tight muscles, throwing full crates, singing a chant, swinging together in a sort of easy tension like a juggling troupe, seeing how long the rally can go on before someone makes a mistake. When they did, a quick breath of laughter before they were back to the concentrated confidence of the game.

Women often gather in groups to pound maize or manioc, which is hard work, but they laugh and chat and sing and have fun. I saw ten men beating coffee beans with big sticks. They stood in a circle around the pile of beans and sang a rhythmic song, one man leading and the rest answering in unison to the beating of the sticks. Like watching a band or a dance group; all the sticks raised then brought down together. It was quite something to watch and I'm sure as much fun to do as banging the drums. This is, I feel, an important difference between this culture and our own, where work is regarded as something separate to life and often not to be enjoyed.

And again, the music. At home Radio One can often be heard crackling inanely from workplaces to distract attention. Do your job with your hands but send your mind off somewhere else. To try to enjoy actively the fact of not being a part of your work can surely not produce much satisfaction or, indeed, enjoyment at all. The work songs found in Africa serve to concentrate the mind on the job, make it easier and more fulfilling. In some respects we've come back to where I started – in the workshop talking about craftsmanship, but it doesn't need to be creative to be satisfying or, indeed, artistic in the true sense of the word.

The red earth roads are cut with deep gullies from the frequent heavy rains. Driving is slow and tedious both for myself and my passengers. The bridges are wooden and sometimes rotten. In England you wouldn't be allowed to drive a car over them but here the local overloaded trucks thunder over them without a care, sending bits of wood flying.

Habitation is almost continual along the roadside – round or square windowless huts, red wattle and daub walls and thatched roofs. The children run out and wave and shout enthusiastically. The adults, too, often smile and wave. Sometimes there'll be a bunch of bananas or a smoked monkey hanging on a stick by the road. This is for sale. It's really only recently, after spending all this time in Africa, that I've been able to appreciate and, to some degree, understand that most of these people have *no money*!

"Well, of course" you may say, but just think about what that means and then maybe you'll begin to understand something of the people and the culture here.

The people of Zaire are not hungry. In fact they are extremely rich in terms of food and the labour required to obtain it. On my previous trip I was impressed by the resourcefulness of the people. Now I see the necessity and inevitability of that. A mud-walled, thatched hut needs no money for its maintenance, neither does a mud road necessarily, or a pit-latrine. Sam commented that you can tell the difference between an African town and a village; the towns are very dirty and the villages very clean. Usually this is because the towns have western-style buildings and paved roads. All western products, it seems, need money for their continued existence, even down to the bicycle. When the tyres split what do you do when you have no money? I've seen the answer in Malawi – you sew them back together again with strands of plastic from old sacks. Unfortunately such ingenuity is hard-pressed to cope with deteriorating colonial sewage systems, communication systems or buildings, for the government are usually as broke as the general population.

We arrived in Lisala on the Zaire River after having frustrating problems with dirty diesel blocking the filters, followed by a fractured brake-pipe which I eventually had to shorten and re-flare after the supposed high-pressure coupling I first used to replace it blew to pieces when the brakes were applied. Anyway, it should be okay now.

Lisala is a strange, one-horse town with a kind of incomplete and empty feeling to it. The infamous Zaire River Boat (see last year's letter!) was, I was assured, due in the next day. I didn't believe it for a moment. Two of my group, Oliver and Karl, have developed high fevers and vomiting, so we had them checked out for malaria... both negative. We drove upstream to Bumbar, which is slightly larger than Lisala and about a day away. Here we were told that the boat would be three days. I heard of a cargo boat leaving the same day, so bought everyone tickets. There was much discussion and some people were a bit disappointed, though I knew that the experience of a cargo boat is hardly less than that of the so-called market boat.

"Ah, but the engine is being repaired!" said the captain, "but it will leave at 4pm."

All aboard at 4pm...

"Well, maybe 6pm. Are you a mechanic? Perhaps you should go and see for yourself, you may even be able to help."(!)

"The boat will leave at 3am."

So everyone slept on the barge under a fifteen-foot square roof with open sides. Sam, myself and two hitchhikers found a factory yard, gave the guard a few Zaires and had a secure spot to sleep in. It's always worth finding a couple of passengers for this section as the roads can be so bad and we may need some diggers. We'd met these two Germans in Lisala, both travelling independently; one had spent sixteen months in Africa, mostly on a bicycle which he'd since sold. He'd worked in Togo and then ridden the bike through Benin, Nigeria and Cameroun. Since then he's been travelling on the top of trucks which is the nearest thing to public transport here. The other guy, Andreas, an anthropologist, had flown into Bangui, made his way to Lisala, crossed the river in a dug-out canoe and spent a further two days on a truck until the road ended. There he'd found a guide and, for his services, bought him a gun without which he was advised not to go where he was going. Next came a two-day trek through the forest to a big river, a five-day dug-out canoe trip, then a further two days walking which brought him to the remote pygmy tribe he'd been seeking. He'd lived for two months amongst these people; eating what they ate, sleeping where they slept and hunting every day. These are not the pygmies of Epulu where I've seen them. They're of a different tribe with a different appearance. They hunt with longbows and spears ten feet in length. They wear no clothes and, instead of using old scrap metal for their spears and arrowheads, which is not an option for them – there being no villages nearby, they actually smelt their own iron. I feel these people to be my living ancestors and it sometimes frustrates me to meet people like Andreas. Now I feel like the ill-informed tour guide that I am. It seems that, like my French, the more I learn about Africa, the less I realise I know. Anyway I can't grumble. Maybe there'll be time to live with pygmies one day myself if I still want to when I get home.

Tourism – like I said, I'm an ill-informed tourist guide and sometimes I love it and sometimes, like this last week, it makes me curl up. Take the pygmies at Epulu for example. They're not the same ones I've seen before and these buggers are really out for what they can get! It makes me cringe to see people making them pose, buying overpriced bows and arrows or dealing out sweets or, worse, cigarettes to them. I sit in the cab and try to forget it's happening. Try to think that if it wasn't me it'd be someone else driving this truck But I can't live like that for long and I know it. Some trips have been expeditions but it's largely up to the groups. This group is predominantly tourists who want a guided tour of Africa with as little hardship and as many photographs and souvenirs as possible. It's my job to make sure they're not disappointed – though I do confess that I relish thrusting hardship and adventure on them sometimes!

Now, back to that boat moored off Bumbar docks for the night. At about 11.30pm we heard the steady 'pok, pok, pok' of the beginnings of rain on our plastic cover and soon, like a Geiger counter at Chernobyl, the noise was so deafening we couldn't even hear each other's chuckles in the truck as we imagined our companions on that open metal deck. The lightning lit the wild, gushing rain like still photographs and the thunder boomed and the wind whipped, frenzied, against the truck. "I hope that boat leaves before morning" I said.

By morning the rain had stopped, leaving huge, opaque, brown pools in the potholes. The boat was still there!

The four of us found a cup of coffee and went apprehensively to the docks. Some of the group were walking around and I met them first.

"Here have a shot of this brandy." One of them offered. "You're going to need it if you're going to face the rest of them."

"Oh dear, did you get wet?"

"Did we!"

And they proceeded to rehearse the first performance of a story that will be performed many times during the next years of their lives. The distant lightning – the knowledge of what was coming, but the sleepy lethargy – the sudden wind, the first raindrops. The feeling, short-lived, of security for those on the down-wind side. Then the lashing torrents. The flash flood carrying all that floated. Soaking sleeping bags. The retreat to a dark metal cupboard, to sleep in grease and old fish and sacking.

Some, to my relief, had actually enjoyed the experience but many were not happy.

"After all, if this had been the 'proper' boat, none of this would have happened" they implied, snugly wrapped in their first-class imaginings. It's actually not so; it would probably have been far worse. There are over seven thousand people on that boat and I was only going to book one first-class cabin *if* there was one available, so most would have been on deck, albeit the first-class deck. But they weren't in any mood to hear that so I didn't say it.

I had a chat with the mechanic and watched the re-assembly of the port engine with interest.

"9am," he said, "we leave."

So we all went to the cafe for a drink which eased things a bit. Now the market boat is due in tomorrow so there's some pressure to wait for it. I know how unpredictable all this is but they do not and still believe what they're told. I hear from a Portuguese man that it won't even *arrive* until Monday, which is another four days, and who knows when it will leave.

Eventually, at 4pm, the cargo boat left. An enormous conglomeration of thirteen barges and one power unit. Three days, he'd said, upstream. My estimate was rather different and I think we'll have a holiday in Kisangani! It takes three days to drive and the sooner we get there the more time we have to ourselves.

We got to Kisangani with no problems and soon heard that twenty-one people have died of cholera on the market boat, which will now remain moored off Bumbar, forbidden to land for three days as a result. So it looks like we caught the right boat after all.

Sam and I had a day-and-a-half's rest before they turned up at the Hotel Olympia one evening. I got a real unnecessary mouthful from Karl, who'd had a fever when we left them but since recovered, for not spending all day waiting by the docks so that I could give them all a lift 1½ km to the hotel (and I'd been worried about him!).

Martine, the French woman, left us in Kisangani. She's not been too happy in the group, though had tolerated it well I thought. I liked her and we got on well. I've since heard that she's bought a pirogue (dug-out canoe) with an Englishman and was having lessons prior to paddling off towards Lisala, Bumbar or, who knows, even Kinshasa. Good luck to them anyway.

Anna got off the boat, having developed another of those dreaded boils. This one was the worst yet and so she and Dr Viktor, her boyfriend, found the elusive Spanish doctor and got it cleaned out; it was the size of a tennis ball on her thigh! They stayed behind in Kisanagani and flew to Goma where they rejoined us today. She and Dr Viktor look like they're set up for life and, before she left, Martine said she wanted a picture of their children!

Jonas left us in Bangui as he was only on that section of the trip. A lot of others had found him hard to get along with. If he thought somebody was taking the mickey he'd ignore them. Some said he was an unwilling worker though he was an intense keep-fit enthusiast – long runs, push-ups, etc. He ate heaps of food yet remained skinny and frail-looking. Underneath he was warm and friendly but, to many, he was aloof and distant.

Cynthia, our Aussie, is one of the liveliest go-for-it people and is always helpful and easy to get along with.

Sophia is usually good fun, especially when it comes to partying, but can do her share of whinging at times. She's not having much luck recently after tearing a big toenail right off and leaving a jigger (a species of flea eggs which are often laid in bare feet) for five days before finding it had gone right under a toenail.

Philippa. No problem at all; helpful, easy-going and never whinging. Always happy to do whatever we're doing.

Emma, again, easy-going, good party person. In fact, all these English girls have a lot more 'go' than most of the others in the group.

Ida, group hairdresser and masseur. Still good fun but occasionally gets a bit fed up.

Michelle doesn't say a lot but makes up for it in thinking. She knows what she wants but, when she doesn't get her way, she lets her position be known, then usually goes along with the decision without complaining. It doesn't mean she's happy, though, and she can be a bit off-hand with people when she's not. She's still keen, with the air of an 'advanced' girl-guide.

Freja is still quiet and shy but usually friendly and amicable which makes up for her boyfriend, Karl. He's the most usual pain in my neck, or, more often, my ears! He challenges everything, every decision, no matter how unanimous. He expects me to run the trip single-handed without any mishaps, unforeseen occurrences, or help from him. On the occasional evenings we have music playing on the cassette player you can be sure that he'll ask for it to be turned off by 10pm (even on my birthday), even though he spends most of the day asleep in the truck. I'm sure he needs all this sleep in order to dream up the next day's barrage of impossible questions. Luckily he hasn't much support from the others. He's not all bad, however, and I can sometimes manage to have a one-to-one conversation with him. I wouldn't like to be their next-door neighbour, though. Since Nigeria he's been treating Freja's boil twice daily which I'm afraid has really spoilt it for them.

Ella and Oliver are still good solid members of the group. Ella has been great, always helpful and always sensible. They both get on equally well with everyone, though Oliver can get a little over-concerned with trivialities, especially since his two-week illness that left him very thin and weak.

Alan, our teetotaller Scotsman, is also a good group member, although, like Oliver, and indeed often with Oliver, can sometimes become worried over trivialities, usually firewood or charcoal (they've bought a charcoal stove). He formed the 'Tea Club' and is a fanatical tea drinker. I still find him one of the most interesting people to talk to, intellectual and scatterbrained!

Mats. Dr. Mats the knife. The primary medical opinion aboard. He's not too familiar with these tropical complaints though, so often I feel as well qualified as him. Also, obviously, he doesn't like to commit himself or make decisions on people's health so he usually advises them to go and 'see a doctor', which is probably why this trip has become a tour of African hospitals, missions and clinics. In many cases, however, I can see that this has been the right decision.

Marcus, a good guy, never a problem, easy-going and gets on well. Always energetic and fun and doesn't complain.

Carol. Unfortunately she's been sick for long periods so has seemed dull and lifeless. When she's well, however, she's unceasingly jovial and witty. She knows plenty of good group games and is always in for a party.

Mille is still quiet and withdrawn or so it seems to the English speakers. Amongst the Danes, however, she's lively and laughing. Though one of our less adventurous members, she does her work and is usually happy to go along with whatever's happening.

Katrine. Always seems to look miserable and hard done by. She snaps back or sighs loudly when she has to do something and often cops out of activities. She hasn't seriously lost her temper that I have seen but always seems on the brink.

And, lastly, Sam, my trainee. He's great. Always keen, sensible and has been a genuine help to me. We get on well which isn't always easy in our sort of relationship or proximity. I don't need to run around after him or check that things have been done. He gets on with it and I let him. He really is Mr Nice Guy – a bit of a shame in some ways to think that he probably won't be like that in a year from now! Still, I'm sure it's better to gain a realistic attitude as long as one stops just short of cynicism!

Inevitably there has been the formation of cliques within the group as a whole but they have not been exclusive and I'm pleased to say that there have been no destructive splits in the group whatsoever. As group leader, though, I tend to be bit more insulated from any wrangles which I find out about, usually through Sam.

Well, last week I met another driver who told me that the Ugandan Prime Minister had been shot three weeks ago and it was a bit unsettled there. I changed my plans to cross Burundi and Tanzania instead. On arriving in Goma, however, nobody knows anything about the supposed assassination. The British Consul said (in French) that there definitely had been no shooting and that is was unfounded rumour. Apparently the Ugandan Prime Minister had left the country about a month ago and there was speculation that there may be a coup d'état in his absence. There was not, and we're assured that it's as safe as it's ever been to cross to Kenya which makes us right on time instead of five days late. We've met several travellers coming the other way who say they've had no problems.

The group, minus wimps and sickies, are probably just about at the top of the Nyiragongo volcano by now. I'd love to have gone with them but I had to drive back to town. Anyway, the new plan means I'll be able to see the gorillas at Jomba which are supposed to be better than at Bukavu where I've been before, and also, possibly, the elephant caves at Mt. Elgon in Kenya.

Till then... hope the summer's turning out to be a good one.

Love,
Graham.

Ngorongoro Crater, Tanzania.
8th June, 1987

Dear All

It certainly feels like a long time since the last letter, so much has happened I'm not sure where to start.

I'll start by mentioning the large amount of high profile cigarette advertising in Zaire. Fleets of smart four-wheel drive vehicles and smartly dressed people, all in the company colours zoom from one town to the next leaving a trail of stickers and peaked caps. The worst culprits seem to be 'Embassy' in their French manifestation of 'Ambassade'. I suppose with the tailing off of cigarette sales in Europe, they feel they have to exploit new markets. Many Africans don't smoke, they've never had the need to budget for expensive commercial brands when local tobacco would suffice if they did indulge. I find it despicable that such an effort is being made to force these people into addiction they can ill-afford in terms of health or money when we are on the verge of eradicating it in our own society.

In a similar vein, we've also seen many instances of dangerous agricultural chemicals, including DDT, long since banned in Europe, though still produced there, openly for sale here. The results can be found in the markets where vegetables may sometimes be covered in easily visible films of unknown chemicals.

And so to Jomba. It has only recently becomes feasible for groups such as ours to visit gorillas here as they previously took a maximum of only six people per day. Now, however, they've just 'habituated' another family, meaning that it's now possible for them to take twelve - six per family per day. I was pleased to have the opportunity to visit them here as it's reputed to be the best viewing of mountain gorillas in Africa, indeed the world. It's also relatively hard to get to, which adds to the attraction.

The first 20kms of the approach roads are rough and steep but nothing too serious. The last 6kms starts narrow, with slippery mud and deep ditches on either side. One false move and we'd be here for a week! The last 2kms is a goat track; deep mud; lots of digging to be done and persistent rain, making it steadily worse. Then there was The Bridge. I walked on and there was an excellent camp spot another kilometre up to 'road'. To go back would have meant reversing 2km back through the mud holes. So,...

"Everybody out!"

It was only eighteen inches wider than the truck and I braced myself against the possible ensuing impact should the bridge collapse. It never came, thankfully, but I did slide into a deep mud hole on the other side which took a lot of work to get out of and was to cause us further problems on our departure.

During our three day stay many local people brought eggs and vegetables to sell and we were even offered a pig!

The Park Headquarters is a further 2kms of steep, uphill walking from the camp along narrow paths, through the fields of maize and potatoes. The two gorilla groups may have been 'habituated' but this does not mean, in any way, that they are 'tamed'. They are simply visited daily over a period by park employees until they tolerate the presence of humans without seeing them as a threat. In the beginning the dominant male 'silverback' can be very aggressive, though it's usually just a lot of noise and chest thumping.

Marcel's family is the original one to be visited by people and he is easily the more placid of the two. Oscar's family is the most recently habituated and he can get quite upset at all these strangers continually tracking him down. Over the time we were there we were split into groups to visit one or the other family. I went to see Marcel. It took about forty minutes with our guide hacking a path through the jungle until we found the trail eaten by the gorillas.

And soon enough we were sitting amongst them. The young ones playfully rolling next to us and trying to steal the guide's hat. The females were plumply sitting chomping leaves or picking nits out of the babies' fur. And Marcel himself, lying on his back relaxing. He just twisted his head around to look at us as we arrived and, for a while, chose to ignore us. The guide took us closer. Now he decided he had to come and say 'Hello'. He rolled over and stood up on all fours before bounding heavily up to us. As we'd been told, we crowded tightly behind the guide. He and Marcel were face to face. This gentle 550lbs bulldozer looked at us and checked us all out in turn and then put his giant hand on the guide's shoulder and shoved him lightly backwards. The guide deliberately fell onto his side. This is a ritual practiced every day and serves to reassure Marcel that he's still the boss! After this he lay down once again to eat leaves and play with one of the youngsters.

It struck me what a lazy life they have. All they need is within arm's reach, lying down and lazing around all day, perhaps occasionally strolling on a bit to find a new spot. All that intelligence; for what? I do wonder what they think about all day. Do they get bored or do they sit and meditate and ponder as to purpose of their existence? In any case, it's hardly surprising they've never developed further, having it so easy. We all have to find enough to eat, though, and if you can find fulfilment in this most basic need, what more could you ask for, what more could you possibly need? Perhaps this is, indeed, the purpose of existence and man alone has come to ponder it because he alone has forgotten it. It is, perhaps, mankind's ingenuity in searching for easy ways out of the hardships with which he has often been faced that has led to our further development. In this way maybe our instinctive desire for the easy life has been our blessing, indeed, our saving grace. Though, if it has, it has also been our curse, inducing us to look no further, using our cosy situation to hide from unfulfillment and only very rarely taking hard, although perhaps more worthwhile paths, when we are already cruising comfortably down the highway.

But back to our now much wetter goat track. We got back to the bridge with little difficulty but, just as the front wheels were almost on the bridge, the whole truck slid sideways into the shallow gully at the side of the road. With much digging and encouragement from the locals I managed to reverse and try again. We threw loads of rocks into the mud but, at the same spot again, it slid sideways. Now, as well as a danger of breaking the bridge, we had the added possibility of sliding sideways off it!

After another hour of road-building I tried again but had to drive closer to the right-hand side than I'd have liked. The wheels would have to run on the edge – and that consisted only of a six-inch diameter log! The spectators amassed. Sam stood on the other side to guide me across and I took several deep breaths and tried to visualise myself driving successfully onto the terra-firma fifteen feet away. Sam beckoned. Four wheel drive and second gear, low ratio engaged. I pushed myself firmly back into the seat against the steering wheel and wondered how violent would be the kick up the backside should we fall. Slowly I crept forward. The logs were covered in mud and apt to be forced apart by the wheels. Sam beckoned with his fingers. The front wheels now halfway.

Rushing adrenaline.

Fluttering leg muscles, tense on the clutch, careful on the accelerator.

Waiting for that slip.

I felt it.

The back twitched and slewed sideways.

I stopped. My guts almost gave up and fell before me.

Sam judged the situation.

I didn't like being on this flimsy bridge so long.

He slowly nodded his head and beckoned. Again I drove. Both axles now on the bridge.

"Go for it." He beckoned with a long sweep of his arm.

Front wheels off now. Power on. The engine roared. The bridge shuddered and groaned as the six-ton rear axle clutched and pulled at the slippery logs. The truck lurched and rocked violently but now happily as we splashed through the deep puddle on the far side of the bridge. I surfaced, breathless but victorious after what felt like three lengths underwater.

The next 6kms to the 'good' road took the rest of the morning; digging and pushing and tightrope-driving on the narrow, greasy-pole track with deep yawning ditches to aid my concentration.

And then, a little apprehensively, we were in Uganda. The scenery in the western highlands was of dramatic steep rounded hills completely terraced and cultivated, unlike anything I'd seen before. People are friendly and officials even friendlier but it's not without a bad taste.

We camped that first night at a police station (better that than having the police come across us unexpectedly in the night). In my anxiety, I'd forgotten that we'd crossed a time zone, so when we got up early to get a good start, it was an hour earlier than expected and still very dark. I decided we'd leave in any case. On the lonely road we were the only vehicle travelling east. The vehicles we saw travelling west were in convoys of fifty or more. No-one had told us we should be travelling in convoy and it was a very tense few hours' driving, hyper-alert to any signs ahead of a possible ambush.

Later we stopped at Masaka, a town devastated by the Tanzanians when they ousted Idi Amin. The twisted concrete still slopes down in undignified heaps. Roofless buildings sport football-sized shell holes and 'bullet-pox' has left the town crippled. The roads are dreadful and, apart from the usual maze of deep potholes, sometimes have extra lines of holes strafed by fighter planes. These probably were aiming at the several now rusty tanks left abandoned by the roadside eight years on. Military check-points are now, thankfully, not too frequent and we only passed about ten as we crossed the country. They're usually polite and friendly but always carry sub-machine guns and have heavier arms at the ready. Often these soldiers are between eight and ten years old! They are fully armed with the legs and sleeves of their uniforms rolled up so that they fit.

These, more often than not, are the sons of the thousands of people killed during the past ten years. Displaced, nowhere to go except the army, they must feel that they've landed on their feet, though they're often used as front-line and 'behind the enemy line' soldiers in the ongoing guerrilla war still raging in the north.

Kampala was surprisingly pleasant; modern, clean and green, though again, most buildings have bullet holes. Nothing like N'djamena in Chad but, like there, the guns seem to have been fired indiscriminately or often just for sport, shooting the windows out of tower blocks being the most obvious example. Every night gunfire can be heard. We camped in the grounds of a hotel near the extensive golf course. Two weeks earlier a gun battle had gone on most of the night on the golf course. The papers said it was between police and robbers but no-one really seemed to know and many didn't believe it. Some people I spoke to thought they were doing it just for fun! This theory was borne out after speaking to some European diplomats who admitted not only to being, of necessity, armed to the teeth, but also to splurting off a few magazines into local trees, or into the air at parties.

"Because no-one cares," one of them said. "Anyway, it lets possible intruders know we're armed." But I caught a strange, boyish, pleading glance in his eye as he justified himself, that said he knew it was bad and he'd just got caught up in this crazy scene like everyone else and was even making it worse.

The country runs on rumours and bad stories and, in Kampala, you'll hear one a minute. I've learned never to believe the rumours until I can find out for myself, though to always believe the bad stories to avoid finding out for myself!

One of the notable aspects of Uganda is the money. At the time I was there one American dollar, in the bank, would buy you 1,060 Ugandan shillings, whereas on the black market, it would buy 15,000. As in all countries with a healthy black market, it is necessary to declare all foreign currency on arrival. Of course, you've got to be very rich or crazy to declare all of it! Unlike Tanzania, the black market in Uganda is so widespread and accepted that the rates are even quoted in the newspapers (they call it the 'open' market), and you can apparently change money with customs officials on the border – though we didn't risk it.

The problem, as far as Ugandans are concerned, is that their jobs only pay the equivalent bank rate value in shillings but the prices are all based on black market rates. This means that, unless you are an employer or farmer, it is impossible to live on your wages. A week's pay, in many jobs, would buy only a couple of beers, and a month's rent is maybe three years' work! This forces everybody to have other, illegal, means of income, usually wheeling and dealing on the black market. I changed $350U.S. and received 5,250,000 shillings! Luckily they've recently introduced the new high denomination 5,000 note! Before, the biggest was 1,000. I still needed a carrier bag. I did have 1,500,000 in 1,000 notes and one night the twenty of us had a meal at the hotel. I had the carrier bag between my feet until it was time to pay. People don't count notes here, but wads. The waiter ended up with six piles six inches high.

Whilst in Kampala it was announced that, on the following Monday, the currency would change - new notes, fewer zeros and a 30% conversion tax. The banks closed and prices went up every hour. We asked the price of food in a cafe and were told to wait until they re-wrote the menu. Coca cola went up three times in one day, eventually 150% more than it had been. Black market rates soared to 20,000 shillings for a dollar, and dollars could be easily spent unchanged. On the Sunday before the change-over we were advised to leave Kampala as there were fears of riots over the 30% tax. This, despite rumours that the Kenyan/Ugandan border was closed and that rebel fighting had extended to within 20kms of the road east. We took the advice and were relieved to reach the border without incident and to find it closed only to Ugandan nationals and freight due to serious tension between the two countries.

And what a relief to be once again in Kenya; like coming home! Mount Elgon National Park is one that I'd long wanted to visit. It is particularly well known for the unique phenomenon of elephants going deep into caves here to scrape salts off the walls. Unlike many of the Parks it is actually permitted to walk around. The afternoon of our arrival, we left the campsite en masse to walk the 4kms to the nearest cave.

"Wow, I hope we see some elephants," I heard one of my group say.

I, however, was hoping very much that we didn't! There are also buffalo here which are probably worse. Still, we saw nothing more dangerous than gazelles and Colubus monkeys. Nor did we see any elephants at the caves, though plenty of evidence was around that they'd been there. The bats were worth a visit by themselves. Tens of thousands, like screeching children swirling confused around in the darkness.

The following morning I drove the truck back to the first cave and then we all walked the 2kms to the second. After this, the group walked on whilst I walked back to get the truck and catch them up. About halfway back there was a stumbling crashing beside me and a large surprised animal blundered through the undergrowth. I couldn't make out what it was and was only glad that it was running away. It ran into the road ahead of me, then stopped abruptly once it saw my meagre size. About thirty feet apart we'd both stopped and were each sizing up the threat of the other. Before me stood what I later discovered to be a 'giant forest hog', like a wild boar the size of a commercial breeding sow; black, bristled and tusked. I half turned round but there was nowhere to go; the truck was on the other side of this obstacle. For several uncertain seconds we stared into each other's eyes before he turned rigidly away and gallumped purposefully into the bush.

"Whew!" I picked up a stick and walked cautiously past the spot where it had vanished. Thankfully, it had long gone.

One thing I did notice, now walking amongst wild animals, was their scent, which is very strong. We may have a poorly developed sense of smell but I think that we often just don't get the strength of smells apparent in the wild. Elephants and buffalo are easy to identify, as are Pygmies or Masai. It's not that they never wash, but African people have a strong scent that is different from that of a white man. Pygmies have a different scent, easily discernible, from that of other Africans. Masai have another and this has continued to preserve them and their cattle from attack by lions since the days when every young man had to kill one as part of his initiation into manhood. They're not supposed to do it now but the lions still remember and stay away from Masai.

I left Sam and the truck and caught public transport to Nairobi. The 'Matatus' - Peugeot pick-ups fitted with a small bus body - won't leave until they're overloaded and, to this end, they'll spend an hour or more revving their engines, blaring horns and trying to drag people in off the street; sometimes grabbing people's luggage and loading it onto the roof before they've even decided they want to go. They usually leave with about twenty people including two or three hanging on outside and their roofs piled high with sacks of maize, bunches of bananas or live chickens tied together by their feet and the like.

The big buses are even more interesting and no less crowded. At regular intervals hawkers will board for one stop; they don't have to pay but sell everything from key-rings and padlocks to samosas, newspapers, Coca-Cola, nuts, cakes, biscuits. Often beggars, usually blind, will get on and sing a song, maybe make a long speech, then pass around a hat. Almost everyone gives something and at the next stop they get off and catch the next bus back. And again, at every town, an hour of revving and horn blaring. They'll edge their way through the bus station pretending to leave, then reverse back when they get too far and start pretending to leave all over again!

I took a room in Nairobi and had myself five days off. To my pleasant surprise I then found that I only had three passengers from there to Harare, two of them from the last group and one new one. Frankie is an Australian woman who's been on our Asian trip. She's easy-going and good fun so the last part should be a holiday.

First stop, the Kenya coast and then a few game parks. We don't need to put up tents anymore and work is easily allotted without a rota or me pushing anyone. For the first time, we went to Ngorongoro Crater, a hundred square-mile area of the Serengeti enclosed by a volcanic rim and teeming with wildlife. It's always been too expensive before, but the price has dropped 30%. It's one of Tanzania's few methods of earning foreign currency. All foreign visitors must pay in US dollars which the government creams off for other things. For five of us and the truck it cost me 210 dollars for twenty-four hours – I'd previously sought permission from London and they'd somewhat begrudgingly allowed me just twenty-four hours here. Although it wasn't my money I must say that it was well worth it! We had an excellent guide who managed to find just about everything the Park has to offer.

After leaving, we found a place where we thought we could camp; a fairly plush tourist lodge called 'Gibbs Farm'. In our book it sounded like an old farmyard where we'd be camping amongst chickens and rusting farm machinery. It turned out that this place is well-known in the 'right circles' and various rich and famous people regularly turn up, including, in 1985, Princess Anne.

They weren't too keen on campers but we eventually came to an agreement and decided also to eat in the restaurant. One of the Tanzanian guys, who appeared to be in charge, had a strangely different accent from the others.

"Where are you from?" I asked, "you have a very English accent."

"I was adopted by English parents," he said, "and I lived in Somerset for quite a long time."

"Somerset? Whereabouts?"

"Bridgwater."

"Oh, I live in Taunton."

"I went to Taunton School!" he said, and he had the most public school accent you could hear and was virtually running the show here as part of his practical training in Hotel Management. He told us that he'd been born in this village and was helping to arrange courses to train his peers in such things as accounting and management techniques where, previously, all they had done was pick coffee.

"It's quite a challenge," he admitted, "for them and for me."

It was during a slight twinge of homesickness, brought on by the similarity of the landscape to Dartmoor and also my fear and apprehension of passing through Uganda, that I decided to list the things from home I missed the most.

I thought of the pleasure of having tea with old folk in their small living rooms full of pictures, clocks and floral settees; home-made scones and delicate cups, always filled before they're empty. I thought of the smell of old books, then of public libraries, then of the history; Iron Age forts, cathedrals and disused canals. Of digging my allotment on a warm Sunday and chatting to the old gardeners. Or of those lazy Sundays; maybe a walk or playing board games with friends. Of evenings of live jazz music, of wholemeal bread, pickled eggs and chips, clean towns, fifteen minutes in the bank instead of three hours, policemen not dressed in military uniforms and carrying sub-machine guns, being able to drink water with complete confidence as to its safety and reliability, and for the excellent medical service that we have, whose staff not only care as much as African hospital staff but have the resources to make the most of all existing medical knowledge, expertise and technology.

I then decided to list those things from home that I didn't miss at all and I found the results rather more interesting...

Television came first, with its deadening influence; the newspapers with their endless supply of scandal and horror that may otherwise never come to concern us. It's good to be away from the ever-increasing volumes of road traffic and its resulting noise that permeates almost every corner of Britain. And motorways, which I accept reduce the volume on main roads and in towns, but it's their impersonality I dislike. The complete disregard shown by them and their users for the countryside through which they pass. And I can well live without luxury, which is not to say that I don't appreciate being comfortable – but without extravagance. Aggressive dogs are something I don't have to worry about here but which can often spoil a walk or cycle ride at home. And, finally, the shyness and lack of openness of many English people, often characterised by a staring at the ground as two people pass each other in the street, and making it less likely that strangers will ever be shown real hospitality.

When I'd finished writing I sat back and looked at all these things and realised that they all really amounted to the same things, and that is our *Insulation*.

And then I saw it, the thing I'd been searching for; the difference between our cultures that makes people here in Africa apparently more able to laugh together, talk together freely as families, sing and dance and work together as communities and, above all, appear, in the face of poverty, sickness and hardship, to actually *enjoy* life and not to fear it. It is that they are forced to participate in their own lives and environment whilst our society has learned to avoid this.

Once we've accepted an easier way of doing something, the feats of those to whom the easy way is not available, start to seem incredible. 'Civilised' people are in awe at the thought of eight year old boys making complicated toy trucks from old tins and wire, or of people having only feet as transport and walking often ten or twenty miles to market carrying heavy loads. Or of living with few possessions other than a bed and a hoe; and bringing up several children on nothing more than they are able to grow. Despite all the advances mankind may have made, in these terms at least, our human potential has been reduced. It is we who are impoverished.

'Dumpt, dumpt, dumpt' came the thumping at the door of my dream. A single snail's eye extended from the safe warm womb of my sleepiness. "Graham, do you know what day it is?" The voice asked at the door. I did and it dragged me reluctantly by the ear back to my small stone cottage in Wales. On sunny days, the dazzle would leap and sing past the shutters but this morning only a grey indistinct blur enhanced the traditional gloom. Alec, though, was bright and springing in his shorts and training shoes. We'd agreed to perform a rigorous exercise programme for an hour three times a week. We'd been doing it now for several weeks and never felt fitter or as ready to tackle anything. But this morning I didn't feel ready to tackle an hour's physical exercise at all. It wasn't only hard work but we'd specifically designed it to be as hard as we could take. I struggled to retain my fast-fading dream that it may transport me back to my previous security in this warm, cosy bed. But I knew I wanted the fitness and, because I was doing it with Alec, I'd blocked my escape. That was the whole idea. We had left ourselves no choice. If we had, I would surely have just kept on dreaming about it. Other days it would be me banging on Alec's door. We'd agreed to limit each other's freedom in order to progress and it worked.

The more I thought about it, the more important participation appeared to be ... We can listen to music without it, but consider the difference when we participate by singing along or dancing or just catching its mood. Without participation its power, its richness, indeed, its very purpose is absent.

We can live in houses built without it but consider the difference when a building is part of its environment through being built from the same stuff of it - or when the builder or architect has put himself into his work. We find the results pleasing and it's hard to believe that this doesn't affect its inhabitants.

And we can survive without it but consider the emptiness and sometimes even suicidal desperation of many unemployed men who've been denied involvement even in their most basic instinct of providing food and shelter. Unemployment could be freedom but, for most, it's imprisonment - not through poverty, for they are far wealthier in material terms than most Africans, but through lack of participation in their own lives. Their resourcefulness and ability to find a way out slips away from them as their lives become too easy and unchallenging. They've ceased to live and a few even lose the will to survive.

I don't believe it's necessary to look back to the Stone Age to discover the qualities realised by participation in our own history. It's not necessary to revert to being a nation of hunter-gatherers or subsistence farmers in order to reap the benefits of being inextricably parts of our own environment. It's open to us all. But, although we may have been changing since we were hunter-gatherers, it was not until very recently that our insulation has become thick enough for its damaging effects to become alarmingly apparent, and especially alarming when compared with peoples who are yet unable to divorce themselves from their surroundings.

In many African communities, Saturdays are set aside for community work. Everyone who is fit and able is expected to partake in such work as the clearing of ditches, cutting grass verges or repairing the church. At home, I fear, these tasks would, to most people, remain forever someone else's responsibility. I heard of a Tanzanian school teacher who went to teach in England and tried to get the children to clean the school on Friday afternoons as they had done in Tanzania. They flatly refused - it was the cleaner's job, not theirs.

As recently as a couple of decades ago in Britain, there was a much stronger family and community life. Older people will tell of the whole village helping with the harvest – or of far more quality goods made by craftsmen or engineers who cared about their work. I'm sure not everyone was happy but I'd find it hard to believe that they were less satisfied with their lot than people are today.

More than any other single invention, I believe that television must carry the bulk of the blame for the state of things in Britain today. A whole nation spending every night numbed and stoned out of their minds, staring mindlessly at the piped images in their 'living' rooms. We'd be justifiably concerned at the effects on society if the whole nation spent each night smoking opium; never quite getting around to doing all those other things they'd like to do; rarely talking with their families or inviting neighbours around. And, worst of all, administering it freely to their children to keep them quiet and so make their own lives easier. So, instead of learning about 'real life', they're already learning the escape route.

The small African woman, with weathered skin and cropped hair plodded barefoot up the steep, rocky road with a huge bundle of firewood, as big as herself, on her head. She smiled at us and mouthed a greeting. Behind her was her daughter, perhaps nine years old, in a dirty, ragged dress and also barefoot. She carried a smaller bundle and, tied on her back with a single piece of cloth, she also carried a baby of about six months. The girl looked brightly up and smiled, though she was unable to turn her head. The baby, however, craned its neck, extruded one arm, beamed a big smile and waved until it could turn its head no further.

It has been joked as to what the newsreader might see should he be able to look out from the television set. He'd see a nation of zombies who'd opted to watch others living instead of living themselves; a nation of families sitting glazed-eyed, still, silent and uncommunicative. A nation of drugged-up children, irritable and uncreative, who'd never really learned to play or think for themselves or relate to other people. It's no joke!

Many people seem to have come to expect to be always entertained. Anything else is tedious drudgery, or unnecessary work. Lack of anything else is a frightening void. That's why I don't think this dreadful notion of increased 'leisure time' can ever produce anything positive. What we need to nurture is *more* involvement in our lives, not more time to escape.

Ah!, would that it were possible to get communities to sing and dance together again. To get families and friends to once more enjoy evenings of discussion, games, music or story-telling. To get children to laugh, entertain themselves and work willingly – but alas, until we give up our addictive 'luxuries' there can be no hope.

Maybe there is no hope. Look at it; in almost every way, people throughout whole of civilisation are sitting comfortably insulated and allowing themselves to be simply spectators of a controlled environment. The thought of 'Real Life', hard, unpredictable and at the mercy of its environment, becomes terrifying. But, like the tingle of excitement when you wake to find yourself cut off by that blizzard, its unexpected intrusion can be stimulating.

Travelling, and especially travelling alone, is throwing oneself completely into it. The thought of effectively relinquishing all control is scary; though most travellers will tell you that, once you've come to trust it – as soon you must – your instinct and its good guidance can be quite astonishing. It forces participation in the moment so, like the craftsman, the traveller or the African bank clerk, there is no more importance in the end result than there is in the moments taken to reach it.

For some people at least, group travel such as these trips, although admitting a wish for adventure, also admits a reluctance to throw themselves into it. Some of them want, in effect, an 'insulated adventure'- a contradiction in terms. I'm expected to provide the buffer between them and the 'Real World' that whizzes past the windows like a boring TV programme. Many of them would never have come to Africa at all were it not for these trips (and that probably also includes me). But they have, after all, implied a desire for 'adventure' by choosing to come on an expedition in the first place. However, when I provide it in the only way I know; by throwing them into unpredictable and often uncomfortable situations – or when it provides itself, with the same effects – I'm in danger of being accused of failing in my duty, which is to maintain this bubble of 'civilisation' they've paid for.

And I sit now at one of my favourite spots: Otter Point at Cape Maclear. The endless drinkable sea of Lake Malawi lays wide to the horizon. Steep, conical mountains and islands, heaps of huge, grey boulders plunge down beneath the splushing waves in an architecture of rounded crevices and balanced meteors. And now the Spring has grown between these elephant hailstones to form a tough and sensitive stiff green rug that soars at pyramid angels, to dress these rude bellies of granite.

The occasional cries of the sharp fish-eagles sound like those of more meditative sea-gulls, whilst breezy fishermen, like free slaves, oar and paddle their tree-trunk canoes through the chop and wave with signal teeth.

Summer, breeze, sunny haze and dazzling definition strike through my shield to envelop me.

And I wondered; could it be that the reason we find such places beautiful, with dramatic or unusual scenery, is because the environment can no longer be ignored and forces itself upon us? Although the people who live in these places are unlikely to consider them beautiful, they shape their lives in other ways as they are forever dominated by, and forced to interact with, their surroundings. Perhaps this would explain the good-natured toughness and resilience of mountain people as compared with people of easier countryside.

Of course, it's not really enough to tell people that they'd be better off if they simply participated in their own worlds. It's a rather abstract statement – I mean, where do you start? Tell that to the suicidal unemployed man and you may well be responsible for his death.

No: it's about our limiting the options and thereby *forcing* participation, not just trying to limit them through force of will; few people are that strong.

For this man, it may mean him selling his TV to force himself to find more constructive ways of using his time. For children it may mean providing fewer ready-made toys in order to force them into creating their own; and, for my group it may mean putting them on an open metal barge in a thunderstorm in Zaire to force them to have a memorable experience and see, maybe, a little more of their own potential.

We have so much in the Western World that is good. We've made so many genuine advances and discoveries which make for a better life, and we have gained so much understanding of our world. I believe that, if we would just re-learn some of the lessons offered to us by the so-called 'third world', we could achieve a previously unattained richness and quality of life.

I know we can live without it, but consider the difference if only we could learn to sing along ...

The end of the journey ... July 1987, Harare, Zimbabwe.

Graham.

_____oOo_____

Map 7e. East Africa and the Rift Valley.

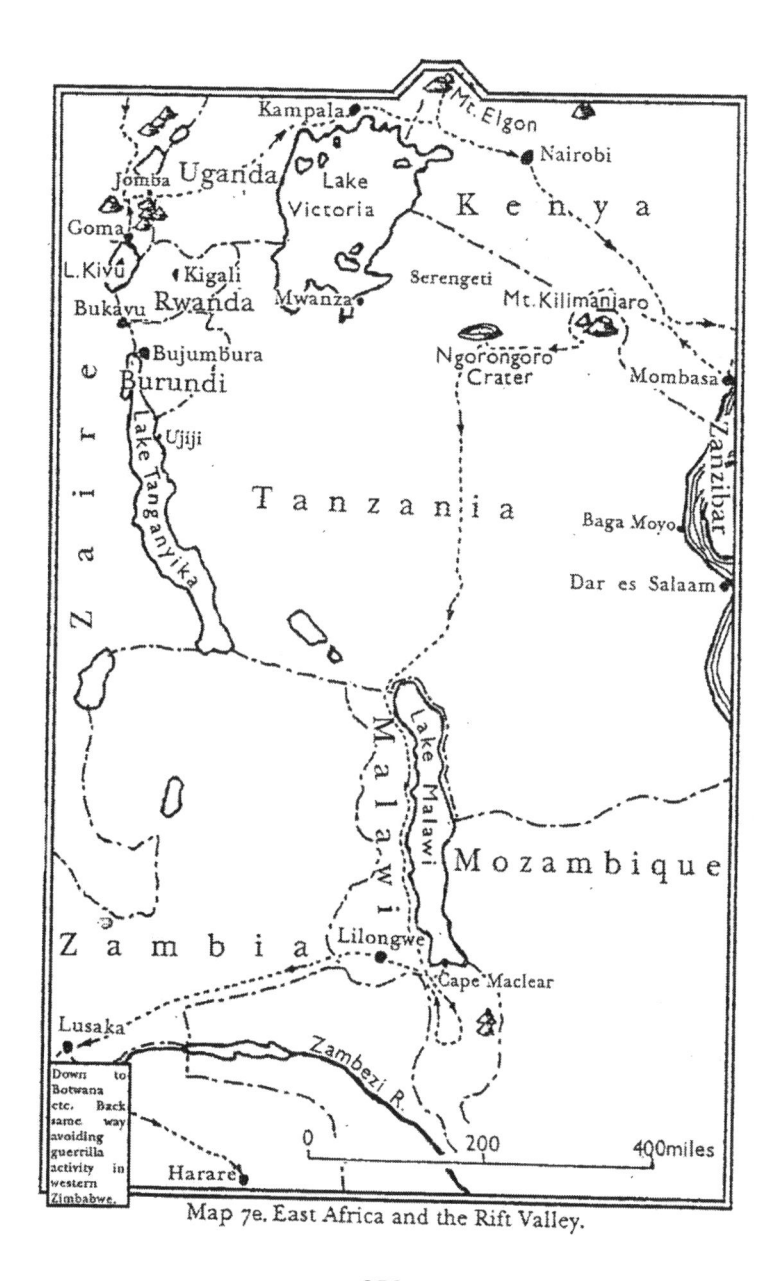

POSTSCRIPT

Having completed my obligatory two years' service with the company, I found myself utterly exhausted. I had given my all and had eventually run out of energy. After my one-trip's notice I was flown back from Harare courtesy of Balkan Airlines. Exodus arranged the ticket – it cost just £150.

It was a coolish summer in Britain. I caught the bus from Heathrow into London to deliver all my paperwork to the Exodus office in Wandsworth. I was astonished at my own disgust at the many bare-chested men I saw in the streets. You'd never see that in Africa – rarely do you even see shorts, except those worn by expatriates.

England, by comparison with Africa, proved to be intolerably claustrophobic. All carved up, all owned, walled, fenced, and tamed. On my second day back, I just had to get out of town. I headed up to a local beauty spot; Lydeard Hill, on the Quantock Hills in Somerset. There were perhaps forty cars in the car-park – bad sign. I set off walking and found myself irritated by a constant stream of people who either overtook me or who I caught up. Clearly visible, about eight miles to the north-east stood Hinkley Point nuclear power station. Suddenly, from nowhere, roared two jet fighters only two or three hundred feet overhead. This was unbearable. I found it incredible that local people – myself at one time – actually came up here for the wide-open space and tranquillity! How they have been cheated, I thought. I left the path and sought the peace of the woods, finding an ancient pollard-oak. I sat down beneath it – peace at last.

A dog came along, or rather a hound, and then, to my disbelief, thirty or forty of them, followed by the entire Hunt, red and arrogant on horseback! It was not only my tranquillity that had been shattered, but also it appeared my ability to feel at ease in my own country. I yearned again for those vast spaces; for that sense of unrestricted possibility that I had so recently taken for granted. The following day found me on a train to Scotland. I spent some time on the Isle of Rhum – chosen because of its absence of roads. Though even here, on alighting from the ferry, I was confronted by a sign listing forbidden activities: camping outside designated areas, fire-lighting, fishing, etc., etc. There's no *trust* here. In Africa you camp more-or-less where you want – respecting village chief's advice in populated areas; you walk where you like – understanding that you don't trample someone's crops; you light fires where you will – being aware of any dangers of it spreading and being sensible about precautions. I'm sure I never saw such signs as this.

Working for Exodus was a hard act to follow. It took altogether five months for me to settle back into life in Britain. I knew I wanted to work with people – particularly, people who needed my help more than the well-adjusted Western tourists I had been used to with Exodus. I also knew that I wanted a period in which to enjoy the benefits of a static lifestyle. There are many things that it is not possible to do whilst travelling constantly; enrolling onto educational courses, for example, or making long-term relationships, or creating lasting works. And so, after five months in limbo, I began work as a voluntary 'co-worker' at the Pennine Camphill Community just outside Wakefield. This involved looking after special-needs and emotionally disturbed adolescents, and helping to run the community's twenty-six acre smallholding. It was every bit as intense and challenging as the expeditions had been, but in an entirely new and different way.

The cultural insights which came into focus in the final letter have also continued to inform my subsequent life, and I have tried, wherever possible, to live a 'participatory' existence. If I am to be honest, however, I must confess that I had already recognised the value of this, and lived according to it, for some time *prior* to my time in Africa – although I would not have been able to put a name to it, or to have framed it in these terms.

I must conclude, then, that, whilst this period did act as a 'rite of passage', it was, unlike more traditional rites, essentially unguided, save by myself. It has ultimately been, therefore, a passage to a clearer understanding of my own nature and my own pre-existing ideas about the world. It is necessary to admit, I'm afraid, that in other cases, there were colleagues who emerged from comparable experiences more cynical, more arrogant and more racist than they were before they started.

GRAHAM BURGESS was born in Yorkshire and moved to Somerset as a boy. Leaving Huish's Grammar School, Taunton, at 17, he went on to be, amongst other things, assistant cartographer, long distance lorry driver, organic farmer, expedition leader, co-worker at a Camphill community, self-employed windpump-maker, graduate in Creative writing, Philosophy and Architecture, independent Town and District councillor and boat-builder. He now runs a small architectural practice in Frome, Somerset.

September 2013

Made in the USA
San Bernardino, CA
02 April 2017